The Little Girl Wins

A Family's Journey Overcoming The Mistakes of the Past

JESSICA STRONG & JIMMIE BRATCHER
with DIANE BRAY

The Little Girl Wins
Jessica Strong & Jimmie Bratcher

Unless otherwise indicated, all Scripture quotations are taken from the Holy Bible, New King James Version, copyright © 1979, 1980, 1982. Used by permission of Thomas Nelson, Inc., Nashville, Tennessee.

Scripture quotations marked KJV are taken from the Holy Bible, King James Authorized Version, which is in the public domain.

Scripture quotations marked The Message are taken from The Message, copyright © by Eugene H. Peterson. Published by Nav Press, Colorado Springs, Colorado, in association with Alive Communications, Colorado Springs, Colorado.

Scripture quotations marked NASB are taken from the New American Standard Bible, copyright © 1960, 1962, 1963, 1968, 1971, 1972, 1973, 1975, 1977, 1995. Used by permission of The Lockman Foundation, La Habra, California.

Scripture quotations marked AMP are taken from the Amplified Bible, copyright © 1954, 1958, 1962, 1965, 1987. Used by permission of The Lockman Foundation, La Habra, California.

The emphasis within scripture quotations is the author's own.

The Little Girl Wins
Printed in the United States of America 2021 by Jessica Strong & Jimmie Bratcher

℗ & © Ain't Skeert Tunes Publishing - Jimmie Bratcher
PO Box 901495
Kansas City, MO 64190

www.jimmiebratcher.com

Editor Diane Bray
Design & Layout Debbie Bishop, dbdesign.graphics
Photo credits Isaac Alongi www.isaacalongi.com & Nikki Bockover

No part of this book may be reproduced or transmitted in any form or by any means, electronic or mechanical, including photocopying, recording, or by any information storage and retrieval system, without permission in writing from the publisher.

Introduction

We have a story to tell. Most people do. When contemplating sharing our story, we wondered: What do people want to hear? What would be valuable to the readers? What would be worth their time? We decided most people would want to read a story that was not only encouraging and uplifting, but was real, raw and authentic. So, the real, raw, authentic truth is, at the very least, messy. Actually, it's very complicated and painful. Can you relate? Are there chapters of your own story that you'd rather have left unread? Many of us would just as soon tear those pages of mess right out of the book. But every page of a story is important and, in our story, there is a Truth that is bigger than our truth. There is a Redemption that makes sense of our mistakes. There is a Love that overcomes our pain and there is a Grace that brings healing to our mess.

We pray you'll find all those things in these pages... and ultimately in your own story, too.

Peace,

Jimmie and Jessica

Acknowledgements

Before we begin, I, Jessica, absolutely must take some time to honor a few very specific people who were present, who stepped into the gap, and just showed up for me for so many years of the story.

My mother, Elaine, is my hero. She is still by far the strongest woman I know. She has lived through more adversity and trial than most could ever fathom or endure. She taught us that family is precious. She always did the best to show us to use our brains, to look around and marvel at the unusual, and that there is excitement and learning in the next adventure. I am so very grateful for her continuous efforts to just keep going no matter how hard life was. Things may not have always gone the way she wanted them to, yet her example reminds me every day to never give up.

My aunts and uncles who drove me places and taught me. They gave me opportunities to see more than just my little space and time. Uncle Randy always had the coolest car and hair. As a second grader at

Franklin Elementary, I just knew I was cooler than anyone when he picked me up in his black 1977 Monte Carlo. Uncle Ron was always the strongest, most fit, and funniest. He taught me that eggs are actually quite strong when you can remember how to do that trick. Aunt Di had a beautifully appointed but humble home. Everything was always clean, orderly, and everything in its place. She showed me a different life and repeatedly made me act like a proper young lady, rising to my potential.

My grandparents, Ralph "Chief" and Charlotte, who sacrificed so much to give me and my siblings much love, stability, and opportunity as was in their power to give, including taking early retirement to help raise us. As the father figure, my grandfather was highly intelligent, incredibly sarcastic and funny. He was bold and loved fiercely and he never met a stranger. There are stories upon stories of how he knew presidents and janitors, befriending them all.

He was the Fire Chief, a machinist, a foreman, and a veteran of World War II. He was a leader to leaders. If you can imagine a six-foot plus Native American man with hands the size of pie plates, eyes black as night and

hair to match. He was an intimidating figure who took great pleasure in food, laughter, Christmas decorations, storytelling, and his family. Grandpa took me to buy my first bra. He took me to buy my prom dresses. He took me to vote the first time. He grounded me for kissing a boy outside the skating rink. He and my grandmother sacrificed their retirement of oil painting and fishing to give my brother and me a different opportunity. My grandparents modeled their value for family first in their lives of sacrifice. They did everything they could to provide stability, love, safety, and absolutely taught us leadership, perseverance, and how to laugh at ourselves.

I hope and pray, Dear Reader, that you will remember these beloved people were ever present throughout all of this. Were it not for them, their love and continuous sacrifice, I don't know where I would be and how my life would look. They together were mother, father, teacher, protector, friend, hope, laughter, and love in all my good, bad and ugly life. Despite my stories and ridiculous decisions, they picked me up over and over. They helped me, wiped dirt and tears from my face, squared my shoulders and held my head up. I hold them in the highest esteem and hope that my stories honor them and the Cottingham name and legacy.

Jessica

Dedication:
In loving memory of
Alice Pauline Strong
September 1940 - July 2019

PART ONE

Memories and Yesterdays

Chapter One:

The Beginning

Jimmie:

I am the youngest of my family and, yes, the most spoiled. I'm told that my parents brought me home from the hospital, laid me in a bassinet, then introduced me to my two sisters. They were not too happy about the arrival of the to-be-spoiled little brother. My parents, Pete and Margie, were wonderful. I grew up in such a manner that I received little or no discipline whatsoever. When I said I was spoiled, I mean it. No, or very little correction, meant that I ruled the home.

You see, my mom had this idea, that was driven by the pop psychology of the day, that taught you should always let a child do anything he or she wanted, without discipline. So, I spent my entire childhood screaming out for someone to tell me what was right and wrong, to teach me good values, to teach me how to act…and nobody did.

Every child needs discipline; it's called love. My dad was a great dad. I never remember a moment in my life where I was afraid of my dad or where I doubted that he loved me. But what I needed most from my dad was for him to grab me by the nape of the neck and to tell me, "No."

As I grew into adolescence I kept getting worse. At thirteen years old I got caught stealing some wheels off a car and was put on probation. Just a few months later I discovered LSD. It became my drug of choice and it was only a matter of time before I was using it on a regular basis. I was looking for an escape; I was looking for a way out. Anything to keep me from facing myself and the reality of who I was becoming. And at that time in our culture, it seemed like it was the thing to do.

As one thing always leads to another, I went blindly down the path from one drug to another. At that time in my life I only had respect for two things: JB Rare scotch and heroin. I had enough respect for those two things that I would not use them regularly because I liked them so much, and I knew it would only be a matter of time before they would kill me. I assumed that I would never make it past 25 years of age. I had this gnawing in my heart that said somehow, someway, I would die. You know, I had some crazy thought like, "Only the good die young."

In 1971 I was a selfish, out of control 17-year-old. I was completely self-absorbed and I made some terrible choices. I was dating a girl off and on, nothing serious as far as I was concerned and one night she came to me and said: *I'm pregnant*. I chose to reject her and accept in my own mind, to be deceived, that the baby she was carrying was not my own. I rejected the truth that I was this girl's dad.

Jessica:

In my first ten years of life, we moved five times. We'd move away from Liberty, Missouri, only to move back again and it kept repeating.

My earliest memories were not of love, joy, or happiness. They were not spinning or twirling in lacy dresses, but I've heard those stories. My first memories are dark. They are full of fear and lack. I remember being very hungry, but knowing I couldn't complain. The house is very dark in my mind. I don't know if it was old or beat up, but it was not a warm happy place...

just dark. An old white farmhouse far away from my hometown.

One night, I don't remember much, but I remember a flatbed appliance truck. Well, I probably only remember a memory that was explained to me over the years. Grandpa borrowed a truck and had come to get us—my mom, my brothers, my sister and me. I don't remember much more than that and the feeling of knowing we were safe now that we were with Grandma and Grandpa.

Every adult at our house worked. I had to go to the neighbors extremely early in the morning. At least in my 4-year-old mind it was extremely early. The neighbor's daughter, Kim, and I were the same age, we were playmates. Her mom babysat me and her dad was so kind to me. He had a loving face and was extremely attentive to my comfort. I don't know that I remember that feeling existing anywhere else in my world then, or for years to come. I do remember wanting to have a daddy like my friends... only mine would be even better.

Mom and me

Sometime between four and five years old, I started dance class. I was a bit of a klutz. I ran into the coffee table, the corner of the wall going into a hallway or the door jamb regularly. I fell a lot and constantly twisted my ankles. Mom decided I needed some help with that. The answer came in the form of ballet, tap, and jazz. Turns out, I loved it and was pretty good at it. Sadly, it didn't help with the falling, running into things or twisting my ankles. (I still do all of them a lot, only in a prettier way now. Recently, I was watching a bald eagle fly over the office building where I work while I was leaving. I rolled my ankle but didn't fall, stumbled and laughed all the way to the car!)

Dance class at the Liberty Dance Center and the Rangerettes gave me many things, but in particular grace and poise. I learned something my mother has always done very well: stand up tall, square my shoulders, don't look at the floor, and walk in like you own the place. That skill, solidified in tiny little ballet slippers, serves me well to this very day.

My ballet shoes

    I remember it was just mommies and little girls at the dance studio. But whenever there were daddy-things to be done, Grandpa came. I remember the stark contrast between me and the other girls; it was not bad, it was not good. It just was. There was something in my heart that began to form. I was different. I wasn't like all the little ballerinas whose daddies came to their recitals. Unmet needs began to bore a deep hole in me.

Dancing became my everything. I am certain I twirled, tapped, and flitted my way through every moment of life that I could. Dance was where I was accepted. I fit in. I was good at it. Mostly, I was free there. I could be whatever person I wanted to be and create any image I chose. I could be fierce and strong, delicate and soft. There were no restrictions. When I danced, I was unlimited. Unbound. Unafraid.

By age six, I began competing and winning with The Rangerettes. By ten years old, I'd won State and qualified for Nationals. Grandma sewed all my costumes, Grandpa built set pieces, painted stools and sometimes drove. Mom often drove me to competitions all over the area.

Dancing with the Liberty Rangerettes

Outside of dance, I had two particular friends, Stephanie and Trisha. We did so much together I felt like I was part of their families. Their houses were so different than mine. Their moms and dads lived together. Their grandparents only came to visit, Stephanie and Trisha didn't live with them. On the weekends, their dads played with us. They laughed, teased, and tickled.

They were so nice all the time. I remember being at Stephanie's and her dad was outside with us. The sun was shining. I don't remember what we were doing, but her dad was smiling and laughing. I remember feeling encouraged and free. We were just having fun... and it felt incredible.

On another occasion, we were at Trisha's. Her dad was home and we were playing and he was laughing. His eyes were so kind and ablaze with joy or maybe just love for spending time with his girl and her friends. I felt so welcomed and so loved.

The feelings of love and freedom didn't last long though. At some point, I had to go back to my reality. I began to ache, wondering why I didn't have a father. And the hole of unmet needs that his absence created grew bigger and darker.

Chapter Two

Transformation and Transition

Jimmie:

In 1973, I met the girl who would later become my wife, Sherri, at a Black Sabbath concert at Memorial Hall in Kansas City, Kansas. Let me tell you, it was a mess right from the beginning. The fighting began and didn't ever let up. I don't remember what we fought about, we just were really good at it and did it all the time.

My response was to do what I knew how to do best, hide. So, I would simply leave the house "to go to the store," and disappear for days or weeks. But for some reason, I would always come back. I felt so connected down deep in my heart to this girl that even though there was great pain, we just couldn't keep our hands off each other. Well, you know how that works... it was just a few months and the announcement came, "I'm pregnant." Those were two words I wasn't ready to hear. But somehow, six months in, we managed to get a license and make an appointment with the judge.

It was horrible. After the birth of our son, Jason, Sherri and I separated but continued to fight. One particularly alcohol-enhanced fight ended with me in the Emergency Room after Sherri kicked in my nose. The next day after surgery to fix it, I was released from the hospital and I went home to my parents' house to recover. At that time my grandmother— "Granny"—was staying there. Now, Granny came in as I was lying on the couch and saw me. She sat down on the couch next to me and said these words, "Baby, I will give you the money if you will just get a divorce." Now you know that your marriage is jacked up when Granny is willing to pay for your divorce.

In a few days, after I recovered, I was off to the attorney's office. Sherri and I split up our few belongings and agreed that we would share custody of Jason. I began to run as fast and as hard as I could into a crazy party lifestyle. I would do drugs and drink like there was no tomorrow, stumble home about four o'clock in the morning, get up at seven and head to work.

All of that time was about one thing: numbing the pain and quieting the conflicting voices in my head. To make a long story short, eventually, the Lord got ahold of Sherri, we were remarried and then the Lord also got a hold of me. (You can actually read our whole story in our book *Granny Paid for Our Divorce*.)

Our lives were transformed, we were set free from the substance abuse, and we had our daughter, Amanda and were loving and serving Jesus.

Several years later, by the mid 1980s after Sherri and I were remarried and born again, and our lives were pretty settled, I was in a restaurant in my hometown and I saw the dad of the girl I dated back when I was 17. He was there with a young teenage girl about 13 or 14. I saw her across the room and she was so beautiful and I knew that she was my child. Sherri and I prayed and considered, we asked ourselves what we should do about this. The answer we received was: Wait. That we should wait. We had a strong assurance in our hearts that when the time came, it was all going to be alright. The Lord really covered us with a special grace during this time that enabled us to wait. Yes, I did think of her often and I would pray for her, asking God to be with Elaine's girl. Beyond praying for this girl who I knew was my daughter, deep in my heart I had this strange knowing that someday we would meet and that somehow, someway we would connect. It was beyond my ability to comprehend how or when but I somehow had this faith in my heart. So I clung to that thread of hope. Someday!

Chapter Three

The Teen Years

We left my grandparents and moved away again. This time my mom, my older brother, my younger sister, me, and my youngest brother, went to Chicago, Illinois, for about a year. Being different from the other girls began to manifest differently now. Instead of pouring myself into dancing, I started to notice boys. They weren't nice boys. When I look back now, I can see they were broken and hurting just like me. Their unmet needs made them predatory. Mine made me codependent and self-destructive. I sought to fill the ache in my heart, to be accepted, loved, and wanted by the daddy who wasn't there. No matter what was provided, the gaping hole I tried to fill grew insatiable.

At twelve, I learned to smoke and drink in the school yard behind our house because I wanted to fit in. I started stealing cigarettes and candy and put on thicker and thicker armor. My poise and grace turned into the mask I could hide behind. Around my family, I could be a generally well behaved sixth grader. At school, I was trying to be tougher and look cooler than I was. Reflecting back now, I know I was hiding and building walls around my heart out of fear, lack and shame. I guarded against everyone. I did make a few friends, yet, I often thought, *"If they only saw what my life is really like, they'd never be friends with me."*

The next summer brought another move... to Tucson, Arizona. My destructive behaviors increased. I learned how to shoplift, increased my alcohol use, and began to dabble with drugs to fit in with an increasingly rough crowd. I was smoking cigarettes all the time, using my lunch money or my theft skills to accommodate the addiction. I got suspended for coming to school drunk at 10 am, and I ran away once. Friends let me hide out and stay in their RV overnight. They thought they were being kind, helping out a friend. But, I was discovered early the next day and returned home.

I couldn't let go of the gnawing differences between me and the other kids. Those feelings left me feeling excluded, kept me from belonging, and caused me to fall into even darker places. I didn't belong because I had no dad. I didn't belong because we weren't from Arizona. I didn't belong because I talked differently. I didn't belong because I .... It was a full-on onslaught of voices telling me I would just *never* belong.

On one particularly difficult day, I came home from school, opened the medicine cabinet and emptied what I could find into my mouth. I thought: *"No one will care. No one will notice if I'm gone. Why would they? I'm not worth anything... especially not worth their attention."* Down the pills went with a gulp. If I had known anything about medication, I'd have taken something besides headache pills and over the counter cold medicine. I ended up with a terribly upset stomach, a very foggy night, and the sad realization, *I couldn't even get **that** right.* My shame deepened.

Simultaneously, my older brother Jim's mental illness began to manifest. We call it bipolar now, but then, no one knew what it was or it wasn't identified by that name. The extreme highs and lows are hard for any parent to deal with, but when you're raising four kids alone, two of them are already off the rails, and you're working 50+ hours a week to pay the bills, I can only imagine how hard that must have been for my mother. I remember Jim was called difficult, rebellious, troubled, and worse. The fighting about what to do about it was constant. The holes in the walls from his outbursts seemed routine. In my 13-year-old mind, all I could think was, *God didn't want him either. At least in that I'm not alone.*

After reasons unknown to me, Jim ended up leaving Tucson and going back to live in Liberty, Missouri, to live with Grandma and Grandpa. My memory here isn't clear. But my heart heard, "*There's nowhere to send you.*" It heard, "*No one wants you.*" I heard, "*See, you're trash. You're not worth anything.*" No one ever spoke these words to me. No one ever implied this. But to that broken 13-year-old, it echoed like loud speakers playing into the Grand Canyon.

Eventually, I ended up back in Liberty, too, only this time it was different. Grandma and Grandpa were home most of the time. They'd retired and were really paying a lot of attention to what Jim and I were doing. This place with them felt safer somehow. Maybe because we were there with them and in that house for so much of my earliest years. I remember I felt relieved and secure there. I remember feeling very special too. We were in church and Sunday school and therapy before therapy was common. They took us clothes shopping, school supply shopping, and it was a whirlwind. I had my own room, it was beautiful. Through my teenage eyes, I saw only home, safety, security, belonging and money, clothes and frivolity. I didn't realize though, how things had shifted.

I was very different. I wasn't able to reconnect

with the friends I had from when we lived there before. I don't really remember why, but I'm certain coming back and looking and acting the way I did, I just wasn't the same girl who's left two years prior. That all meant one thing: *I didn't fit in.* Down into the darkness I went again. My masks got better, more creative and specific for the intended audience. I began to learn to mask who I really was with a certain kind of dominance and a *know-it-all, I-have-it-all-together* persona.

Grandma and Grandpa took us to church a few times and I was very excited to go. But my shame and wrong beliefs didn't take long to manifest. The youth group was fun. But shortly after I started, they went on a ski trip that had been planned long before we arrived back in town. The group's absence the Sunday of the ski trip pushed me over the edge. "I'm not going where I'm not wanted," I told my grandmother. She never made us go back. More shame and regret were piled into my head and heart as my laundry list of places I didn't belong grew. I continued to master my skills at hiding.

I was good at flying under the radar and hiding in the noise of life. I had good grades, I wasn't ever disruptive or disrespectful. I went to school regularly and was on the track team at Liberty Junior High School... at least long enough to get my picture taken with the team. Like everywhere else in my life, I lied to present the image I felt safe showing. I pretended to be on the cross-country team so I could hang out with my new "friends" at the convenience store down the street. I lied about being at practice and stayed at the convenience store hanging out until it was about time to get picked up, then I managed to wander back to the school in time for Grandma or Grandpa to pick me up. No one noticed I smelled like cigarettes or that I didn't look like I'd been at cross-country practice: I still had perfectly coiffed hair and wasn't sweaty from running.

My grandparents trusted me. I would tell them I was going one place and I'd go to another. One of those times, I was at a party. I sat there with a cigarette in one hand, a pint bottle of something in the other. My friend Nikki asked me, "If you ever met your dad, what do you think you'd do?" I exclaimed without hesitation, "I'd punch him in his mother f***ing face and walk off. He doesn't have any use for me, why should I have any use for him?" By then anger and bitterness toward him were all I could muster. I longed for justice and for his punishment. But I also longed for a dad. I told myself

I had dealt with my emotions and feelings concerning this man. There was nothing to say, no reason to say it, and I wasn't going to entertain such silliness. Case closed. Besides, I knew I had Grandpa for all that. I didn't need a daddy anymore. All those desires, longings, and needs were put away in a box in my heart. Secretly though, I longed for my daddy. When I was alone in the deepest part of the night, I wondered what he was like. I imagined Father/Daughter dances and so many other joyful things only to wake up to reality.

I am grateful I had Grandpa. He did so much to fill that need. He drove me to dance practice many nights a week. He drove me to countless competitions, parades, and other events. He even escorted me in a beauty pageant. Miss Gladfest, 1989. I didn't place, but he was there. He sat on the front row so I could see him.

While those moments were precious to me, they weren't enough to keep my patterns of destruction from worsening. I was high or drunk every weekend. I had a girlfriend that I ran with during those days. She and I regularly told our parents/grandparents we were staying at another friend's house... who conveniently didn't have a phone. One night we decided to try to find a party and we were walking all over town trying to find anything, but found nothing. We did eventually find some 40-something guys who were willing to give us a ride into the city and get us high along the way. We were already stoned when they picked us up and then we drove around Liberty for maybe 15 minutes, increasing the high. I had a surprising moment of clarity when I heard something in me say, "Get out of the car." At the next stoplight I told my friend, "We can't go with them. I just remembered there's someplace we have to be." Surprisingly, they let us out and drove away. We slept in the park that night, shivering and scared.

Looking for any opportunity to numb my pain, I began looking for harder drugs, but my brother stepped in. Despite his own severe hallucinogenic drug use, he threatened me and anyone he knew who would give me those harder things. Clearly, I remember when he said to me, "This is not your path, it might be mine, but I'm not letting you walk down it." Nonetheless, my unhealed wounds and pain increased the demand for numbing.

By the time I was 16, I was paying more attention to boys. Somehow, I managed to only have a date or two.

My grandpa and brother were intimidating, so I had to start going out of town to get anyone to pay attention to me. I found one. He never hurt me physically, but the manipulation and emotional games were crystal clear. This became my new pattern: Find some boy to pay attention to me, pursue me, chase me. Then, get my heart broken by their controlling destructive obsession. Rinse and Repeat.

Because of my habit of using drugs and alcohol and relationships to numb myself, any pursuits for a healthy life were met with self-destruction… like my feeble attempt at college after I'd graduated high school. I lasted just over a semester. Then, I moved out of my grandparents' house over a weekend while they were out of town, for what should have been a one-night stand with a guy. However, the damage was done. The bridge burned.

Grandma and Grandpa wouldn't let me come back. I stayed with another girlfriend for a while and she hid me in her garage apartment for months. Then I met the next boy. I followed this one to two different states, only to be left there with his family when he returned to his ex-girlfriend. Broken and full of deeper embarrassment and shame, I came back to Liberty and to another stint in the same friend's garage apartment. After much pleading, my grandparents allowed me to come back and stay with them for two weeks, then I was on the move again...back to Arizona.

Chapter Four

Military Men and Marriage

Jessica:

In 1991, I moved back to Arizona with my mom. I was so broken by then that her attempts to mother me were met with anger, bitterness, lying and defiance. After about a year, she moved due to her job, I stayed in Tucson. I had a job, I had public transportation, I had roommates who wanted to party as much as I did. I had FREEDOM! At least that's what I thought. Eventually the roommates changed, the job disappeared and I ran out of options. My self-destruction met me at every turn, but I was too ashamed of myself to go to Mom. I'm no longer able to go back to my grandparents. Desperate, I walk into the Air Force recruiter's office.

I tested well for entrance and could pick any job I wanted. As I was preparing to leave and was finalizing the paperwork, my grandfather sent me a letter with my birth certificate and other critical documents. His letter said: "I'm so proud of you for making this decision. It will change your life." I carried that letter with me for nearly 20 years before time took it.

The night before I left for basic training in November 1992, I stayed over at this terrible motel in anticipation of ridiculously early transportation to the airport the next morning. As I was standing and waiting for them to plate the most unappetizing eggs I've ever seen, I saw a roach crawling across the upper molding of the serving window. The momentary glimmer of hope I felt when I was accepted into the Airforce disappeared with the roach. Horrid eggs, a crappy hotel, fatigue, discomfort, and the fear of not knowing if I was going to make it through this. I silently believed at that moment: *This is all I'm worth.*

    I was not the best in my flight, definitely not the worst, but I'd survived.

The Air Force

After 8 weeks of training, I was now officially Airman First Class Jessica Cottingham. As I boarded a plane for my next school, I met this girl, Jenn, and we became fast friends. We both looked to be chosen, for validation, and for love, in all the wrong places. We were so similar in so many ways. Eventually, our careers and choices took us to different places. We parted ways after two years of friendship.

In 1993, I thought I was living the dream. I was marrying a soldier. We had great fun and adventures doing silly things, drinking, partying, and working hard. It seemed idyllic. We had a great time until he had to leave for a year unaccompanied in Korea. That kind of separation has the reputation of making or breaking marriages in the military. At that time, there was no email, no texting or Wi-Fi. It was all handwritten letters and occasional, very short phone calls with terrible connections.

Just a short month after he left, I found out I was pregnant. Terribly excited about this beautiful baby, I was not terribly excited about weighing 200 pounds or that my husband wasn't there. My mother was and I am so grateful. She drove me to every appointment, cooked, pampered, and got me Kentucky Fried Chicken mashed potatoes and gravy by the gallon, it seemed.

Thankfully, the pregnancy was easy, as pregnancy goes. Rick was able to come home arriving days before the baby was born. After 14 hours of labor my beautiful monkey, Richard Aaron Yates arrived. At 10lbs 5oz, he looked like a 3-months-old. He was my world before we'd even met, but after he was born, this baby boy was my EVERYTHING. My husband left almost as quickly as he arrived. Postpartum hormones raged. The fatigue of a new baby got to me, despite having my mother's help. All the brokenness and destructive patterns could no longer be met by partying every weekend. The infection continually seeped into every aspect of our lives. I became increasingly disinterested in anything but this baby. By the time he got home from Korea permanently, Rick didn't stand a chance.

While we all bear responsibility to some degree in every relationship, the only good thing I contributed to this one was my body to birth my incredible son Aaron. I was a terrible wife. That broken little girl couldn't love, care for, or nurture that relationship in any safe or healthy way. Rick and I were great friends who got married. It should have been a storybook marriage, but I was too broken.

Within a few months, I kicked him out, and began divorce proceedings. The depression and destruction got worse. My sweet Aaron's beautiful face and my mother's refusal to let me sink further were the only things that kept me from walking down the suicide road.

I still didn't know how broken I was. Life kept going and as the separation and divorce progressed, I began dating. I could not see that I needed deep healing and intensive help. I chose a date and a one-night stand with a neighbor/friend. Every choice has a consequence and I became pregnant again. I was terrified and couldn't see past the destruction having a baby at that time would have caused. I was still active duty and still married; he was very senior to me and we shouldn't have been in a relationship. I was subject to punishment by the Uniform Code of Military Justice if my unit found out

I called him and we agreed that having the baby wasn't an option. He offered to pay for the unthinkable. We made the appointment and went. Walking in the door was surreal. My heart was pounding so loudly I could barely hear the instructions, let alone follow them. I got called back for the procedure, and he went for a drive not being allowed in the room. I was scared, unsure, and at the moment, completely alone, the nurse asked if I'd like to see the baby. *NO! NO!* Fiercely shaking my head, I thought, *Is she out of her mind?* If I saw the baby, I knew I wouldn't go through with it and I'd lose everything. Then the doctor said, "This baby measures at 16 weeks," which meant that it would be more expensive. They wouldn't do anything more without payment, there was no billing option. On the inside, I wanted to run out of that place. I longed to run away and hide from this possibility. I looked around the waiting room to get him, but he wasn't there. Still panicked, I pulled out my credit card, secretly hoping it wouldn't go through… but it did. I went back in, the doctor and nurse came back to get started.

The nurse asked me again, "Do you want to see the baby?"

I can say there are only three times in my life before I became a believer that I'd heard the voice of the Holy Spirit up to this point. Laying on the table in the abortion clinic was the loudest of those three. *"Please look at our baby. Look at this gift we're giving you."* I turned toward the wall and with shame already too much to bear, I stared at the wall and cried silent tears as the baby was ripped out. I can still hear the sounds which haunted me for nearly twenty years.

For any of you who have done this or are considering it, please seek help. Whether through a crisis pregnancy center or post-abortion counseling, you don't have to do this alone.

Thankfully I have accepted God's forgiveness and healing. I have seen visions of my sweet baby girl in heaven, whole and beautiful. Her name is Isabel Grace. And I cannot wait to meet her.

Chapter Five

LeRoy and the Boys

Jessica

October 1997, less than a year later, I was officially divorced and met LeRoy. I remember the very first time we encountered one another. My friend Nancy invited me on a smoke break with her stated intention to introduce me to LeRoy. He and I were both in uniform…I know there's at least one girl reading this book who knows the United States Marine Corps has the best uniform. WOWZERS! LeRoy, in his Dress Blue Charlies, hubba hubba!! For you non-military folks, that's a long sleeve khaki shirt with a tie, dark blue trousers with the red stripe and all the ribbons and devices. We shook hands and locked eyes. Time froze. That moment is burned into my memory unfading, unchanging. I knew there was something very special about this guy.

Twenty minutes later, Nancy asked me again to go smoke. Adamantly refusing didn't really work with Nancy. She was insistent that I meet Lee. I was thinking that this woman is out of her mind. First of all, I have work to do. Second of all, how many guys was she introducing me to in one day? She was relentless and I gave in. We walked out into the courtyard and immediately I felt like an idiot. Lee and LeRoy were the same guy. Nancy was determined that we were meant for each other and we needed to just get on with it.

After a short two weeks, he obviously knew this was a lifetime relationship too. He whispered he loved me when he thought I was sleeping. We dove head first into each other's lives. We met each other's children and became an instant family. We needed each other like our bodies need oxygen.

September 10, 1998, and we'd just finished a family reunion for my grandparents' 50th wedding anniversary. LeRoy came home with Aaron and me to meet the family and celebrate. That evening when all the "grown-ups" had settled into TV or whatever they were doing, LeRoy and me, my three siblings and their significant others went to sit out on the back porch to swap stories, have a few drinks, and just enjoy ourselves. Music was going, LeRoy and I started dancing. Before I knew it, "Will you marry me?" slips out of his mouth. I burst into tears and say, "Yes!" My little brother caught the moment immediately and then the only thing that could happen, happened…. DOGPILE!

We were ambushed—attacked even—and the whole lot of us tumbled in a heap and rolled down the hill eventually coming to rest, all the while laughing and crying and congratulating and just loving our family. The celebration was short but incredible.

I said, "YES!"

I will never forget that moment I met Matt and Seth for the first time. They were perched on the top of a collapsing building with LeRoy. I knew at that moment I was either in big trouble, or we were going to have an incredible adventure for the rest of our lives. I was right on both accounts. I'm pretty tough for a ballerina and an Air Force girl, but these guys are seriously guys, guys. They're both brilliantly smart and ridiculously funny and 100% passionate about everything they do. Life with all these boys has been a crazy ride!

I would love to say I was a perfect mom to them, but we all know those don't exist on this side of heaven. However, I might be one of a few moms who know what a petrified lime looks like, how it got under the furniture, and that one should always keep an eye out for such things when the boys have been home for any period of time. I know why there are underwear on the ceiling fan, pants on the second story foyer window, and the sound a vacuum makes when it sucks up airsoft BBs purchased deliberately in the exact same color as the carpet. I know that I must be incredibly specific, articulate, and think through every possible loophole when providing instructions of any kind that could possibly be misunderstood, misinterpreted or otherwise confused.

Recently, we came home from a date to the island in our kitchen completely hidden under a towering pyramid of red plastic cups. I had mistakenly asked them to pick up a pack from Costco. I am fairly certain I asked them to leave them on the island. My mistake, not asking them to leave them in the package. But I'm getting ahead of myself.

In 1998 we received orders to England. LeRoy left three months ahead of Aaron and me. I had to do some training before we left. Three months later, I was in Survival Escape Resistance Evasion (SERE) School and then went straight to England. Three months later, I am in Survival Escape Resistance Evasion (SERE) School and then straight to England.

We moved in together, just us three, Aaron, LeRoy and me. Matt and Seth were in the States with their mom. Almost as quickly as we got there, I was pregnant. LeRoy adamantly insisted we would not have this child outside of marriage despite our living arrangements. On July 23, 1999, we were married in Cambridgeshire, England, with a small group of friends and all of our boys: Matt was 12, Seth was 8, and Aaron was 3. On our wedding night we got several types of ice cream, made popcorn and snuggled on the floor watching movies with our three boys on the floor around us, and the fourth one waiting to join us.

In February 2000, our Jacob was born, 9lb 9oz of adorable, ravenously hungry, pudgy wudgy, happy baby boy.

Jacob

When the boys were with us during the summer and then permanently, we had so many adventures roaming around the English countryside. We explored Warwick Castle with its knights and armor. We spent days at the Duxford Museum marveling at the World War II planes. We adventured to The Tower of London and Legoland. We lived behind a manor house that was more than 1000 years old overlooking our own orchard where we raced our go cart. We even found the remains of the castle where Mary Queen of Scots was imprisoned prior to her execution. There isn't much there but a sheep pasture, the remains of the castle mound, and 6-foot-tall Scottish thistle, rumored to have been planted by her supporters. And like any good Americans on holiday in England, the boys, LeRoy included, had a battle royale with sheep poop, hurling dried mounds at each other, laughing until our faces hurt and we just couldn't laugh anymore.

It seems almost picture perfect doesn't it?

But that little broken girl was still in there and now she was married to a broken little boy, both of us masquerading, acting like we had it all together. The consequences of all the choices and trauma were still there. Our marriage was on an unstable foundation. He was demanding and I was people pleasing and we were both so insecure. It was emotionally destructive for us all. To make it worse and support the common perception in the military world, our problems must wait because duty called. During this time LeRoy deployed to Pristina, Kosovo, and Sarajevo, Bosnia, I deployed to Iraq and Afghanistan. The Balkans conflict was ending, September 11, 2001, had just happened. Our problems were shoved deep down until the pressure built up. We would have a blowout fight and just put the lid back on the pressure cooker of our marriage. We created a cycle of drinking and fighting and performing our duties as expected. My time in the military came to an end. We moved to the Washington, D.C., area to finish LeRoy's Marine Corps career. Eventually, we both ended up working for the government. Our kids had everything they needed and could possibly want... except emotionally stable parents.

Chapter Six

Preparing the Way

We moved to a new bigger house in 2006 shortly after LeRoy's retirement and our decision to continue to work in Washington, D.C.

I began to explore the feeling I had that there was something missing from our lives spiritually. A friend invited me to her church. At that time, I wasn't strong enough to begin breaking out of my dysfunction. Church attendance was sporadic at best, but I did find some surface level connection with some of the women and I even attended a bible study...my first ever...*What's So Amazing About Grace?* by Phillip Yancey. I didn't fall in love with the church, but my longing and want for more continued to grow.

As we settled in this small and out of the way neighborhood, the kids were settling, too. Specifically, Aaron. There were piles of middle school kids his age, all teenage boys, they were like a swarm of locusts swooping into the house, eating all the food and leaving. We spent many Saturdays and Sunday mornings trying to figure out which kid's house they stayed at the night before.

Some of Aaron's buddies went to a youth group at a large local church and Aaron started pushing, "I want to go to youth group, Mom." Reluctantly, I said yes, but not until I checked out this church. December 2008, I walked into a joint Christmas Eve service of New Life and The Garage. As we were navigating the crowd and nerves, this woman with unmistakable red hair walked in front of me with her hands full, juggling radios.

Instantly, I realize it's Jenn Legacy, the friend I met at the very beginning of my ten years serving in the United States Air Force. I hadn't seen her in many years. We briefly connected and then off she went, as she was the event coordinator for the venue, and about to be a pastoral ministry student and full-time staff member at the same church. That night, I was so excited to see my friend, but the next morning I panicked. She REALLY knows me. She knows some of my worst stories. She knows.

I breathed hard for a few days then I got a call from Jen, "Hey, would you like to get together?" No judgement, no condemnation, just an invitation. As we reconnected, I realized that this is not the same girl I knew. She was still Jenn, but on the inside, she was not even remotely the same. We began developing a new friendship and she began telling me about Jesus. I saw in her a stability, a peace, a transformation I cannot explain. My heart cried out for this.

By the grace of God, she did something that changed everything for me. She invited me onto a leadership team. Most church leaders would be panicking over this. Jenn knew something about me though, she knew I wouldn't come if I wasn't leading. Leading is in my DNA and I think she knew I would have run away if I had to just sit in a pew. What I didn't realize then was that I wasn't really *leading* anything, but I *was* on the team. I served as the gap filler, gopher and I was being discipled there. I found the beginnings of my relationship and love affair with Jesus.

New Life Women's Ministry 2009

PART TWO

Reunion Coming Together

Chapter Seven

Paths Cross

Jimmie:

I was asked to speak at a large church outside St. Louis, Missouri, for their Father's Day service in June of 2009. Sherri and I had been doing traveling ministry for a few years by then, but this was the one and only time I had been to this church. I was playing my music and sharing the story of my life with Sherri, our early years of substance use, our marriage, divorce and remarriage. It's quite the God story, if you've never heard it, filled with God's grace, reconciliation, forgiveness and redemption.

Now remember, this is on Father's Day.

Jessica:

So, on Father's Day, 2009, my sister, Jennifer, was at church near St. Louis, about an hour from where she lived. She was sitting in this particular church, in this exact service. There was a guest preacher that day, a blues man and evangelist. The music was smoking hot. The story was one of restoration, redemption, and healing. Jennifer texted me and started telling me about this tear jerker of a story about a little boy's prayer for his daddy to come home. So she called me after church was over. "Okay," I said, "What's his info, I want to look him up." Jennifer said, "His name is Jimmie Bratcher." I dropped my phone, it took me completely by surprise, I was reeling. I heard her yelling into the phone trying to get my attention. I looked at my phone on the floor and started to walk away, then I came to my senses and remembered she was on the phone. Swallowing hard, I tried to force my heart out of my throat and back into my chest. I picked up the phone and struggled to ask her, "Do you know who Jimmie Bratcher is to me?" "No, he's just this preacher guy from Kansas City," she said.

I choked on the words, "He's my dad." Jennifer wasn't aware that the only things I knew about my dad were that he played the guitar, that he had long curly hair, and his name was Jimmie Bratcher.

My little sister realized the possibility that we could become connected and asked me, "What are you going to do?" That threw me into a panic. I made an instantaneous decision: *I'm not dealing with this. I'm just not. I don't have time for this. My life is complicated enough.* I put it away. I put it into the "daddy" box deep in my heart. I said, "I'm not doing anything. He hasn't been here all this time, why would I care to have that mess in my life now?" That was exactly how I felt. I was so hard hearted about the whole thing. I thought, *"I don't care what he's got! Great! He found Jesus, whoop de doo!"* That was the attitude I had.

For the next eighteen months, the thoughts of this man, my dad, Jimmie Bratcher, kept coming up in my heart. Whenever I'd hear anything about fathers and daughters, see something on TV or in a movie, I had this constant nagging in my subconscious. Yet, I kept going, "Mmmmm...nah, I'm good. I don't need this. I don't want it. I'm not looking for it."

I believe this was a divine appointment, though. You see, I didn't know the Holy Spirit would move in this moment in ways I couldn't have imagined. This moment launched a series of events that took a lifetime to prepare me to receive.

Chapter Eight

One
Less Daddy

Jessica:

At this point I'm two years into my Christian walk and my father-in-law, LeRoy's dad, Eugene, has become a father to me. I could call LeRoy's parents and we could talk. We visited as often as we could manage over the years on an enlisted salary and enjoyed spending nearly every Fourth of July with them. Around 2004, Gene was diagnosed with cardio obstructive pulmonary disorder—COPD. The causes of this disease vary, but he had three primary contributing factors: In his 20s he was exposed to chlorine gas; he smoked for more than 50 years; and he experience prolonged exposure to diesel fumes as a long-haul truck driver for nearly 40 years. There is no cure for COPD. The disease quickly took his ability to travel and chained him to an oxygen tank. In 2009 the oxygen deprivation to his brain radically changed him and he became less and less the man we knew and loved. In February 2010, the ambulance drove him to the hospital for the last time with his blood oxygen at 31%. When the decision was finally made, he was in hospice for less than 24 hours.

We each took turns sitting with him. It was my time with him and I was angry. You know we have those loud moments with God? If I'd been anywhere other than that hospice room, I'd have been screaming because he was dying. Literally breathing his last in front of me.

My grandfather who raised me was almost 90 at this point, it was only a matter of time before every positive father figure I'd had in my life was gone. And I asked God, "WHY?! If you're so good, WHY!? Why would you take them from me?! This is one of the only dads I've ever known and now you're going to take him? How dare you take him from me! Who do you think you are?! *Who's going to be my daddy now?!*" He didn't answer in that moment but in the days and weeks to come, God's answer back was, "You just have to trust me."

When he passed away, in my heart, retired Sergeant Major Eugene Elijah Strong, father and husband RAN into heaven singing cadence. Once he was there, he sat down to coffee with Jesus on the back porch. Because that's just what that old retired Sergeant Major would have loved.

Eugene Elijah Strong

And for the next year, almost every sermon, every scripture, every study, every time I was alone with the Lord, He just kept reminding me, "You have to trust me." I went through this process of *I wonder what it could be? I'm going to get a new car, a new job, or I'm going to move back to Missouri.* I had this whole list of stuff and I said, "Okay, God, here's my list." And I continued to stuff the whole Dad/Jimmie revelation down deep. *Don't need it. Don't want it. Nah... I'm good.*

Chapter Nine

"Trust Me"

Jimmie:

So fast forward to a year later, February 13, 2011. Sherri and I are in Christiana, Pennsylvania, for the weekend doing a marriage seminar, plus I'm preaching three Sunday morning services. I'm in the green room getting ready to walk out to preach the final service when I heard a voice down inside my heart, and that voice said this, "I'm about to change your life." And I knew that voice.

I knew that it was the voice of the Holy Spirit speaking to me, and I started to dream. And I started to think about all of the things that I wanted changed in my life. Like maybe Sherri and I would quit traveling and I'd get a real job. But you know what? We never get it right. Because God's dreams and plans are always bigger and greater and far more wonderful than ours.

I went out and preached the last service and we got in the car and started riding back to Philadelphia to the airport, when I got an email from Jessica's mother. I hadn't heard from her since 1971.

February 13, 2011 at 1:35 PM
To: Jimmie
From: Elaine

I think it's way overdue for you to meet your daughter and grandsons. Her Facebook is Jessica Strong. She doesn't know about you yet.

February 13, 2011 at 1:44 PM
To: Elaine
From: Jimmie

That is wild!!! Wild in a good way. I saw her, your son Jimmy and your dad once at a restaurant in Liberty in the mid 80s and thought that girl looks a lot like me, I would like to meet her. I would welcome knowing her if she is open to that and you're good with it.

I'll get on Facebook and look her up and we can work on the details of making it happen. Thanks.

Jimmie

...So, the first thing I did was to look her up and I sent her a friend request.

Jessica:

But, I did know about my dad. I'd been gobsmacked by the surprising and "chance" encounter Jennifer had in St. Louis, but I continued to bury any stray thoughts. *Not-Gonna-Go-There.*

It was February 13, 2011, fifteen days shy of exactly one year since LeRoy's father passed...since my Daddy-in-law left me. My marriage is not in a good place. My kids are not in a good place. Things are just rough. I was going to check my email really quick, and then hop in the truck and run into town. I checked my inbox and there was an email that said: *Jimmie Bratcher wants to be your friend on Facebook.* And I said, "LeRoy, you need to look at this email." He said, "Woman, I'm watchin' the race." We were watching the Daytona 500... Now, that may not be significant to some of you, but my husband is a big NASCAR guy, he was watching the "Super Bowl" of racing, and I'm interrupting. I said, "No, Baby, you need to see this. It's really important."

I handed him the computer—because Facebook wasn't an app yet—and he looked at it and said, "Isn't he your dad?" I said, "Yeah." And he said,

"What are you going to do?" I said, "Nothin'. I'm going to the store." And in total panic, denial and shock, I got in the truck and went to the store. I don't remember the drive. I'm pretty sure it was by muscle memory that I made it there because somehow I ended up in the store parking lot. Not sure if I went into the store or if I bought anything, but I remember sitting in the parking lot.

My mom sent me a text that said: *Call me.*

I called my mother and she asked me if I was okay.

I told her, "No."

"Really?"

"No, I'm not okay. I'm terrible. I'm terrified."

She said, "You don't have to do anything."

I said, "I know."

"Well, what are you going to do?" she asked.

"I DON'T KNOW! What do I do with this!? What does he want?!" I squawked.

She continued to attempt to console me when I was pretty close to hysterical.

After we hung up, I sat in that parking lot in that truck for the better part of an hour and I cried. I cried because I didn't know what to do. I cried because I was terrified. I cried because since saying goodbye to my father-in-law in hospice leading up to that moment, I'd been asking God: *What are you doing?* God kept telling me: *I got something for you. It's huge. But you have to trust me.* I sat in that truck and I said, "REALLY?!" Remember, I'd given Him my list of approved things He could give me. But, the job, the car, or a move weren't what He wanted to give. I wasn't at all prepared for what happened next.

Jimmie:

For weeks after I sent the friend request, Jessica was silent as she processed the pain of my appearance. For the following weeks I went into what I can only describe as the deepest grief that I've ever experienced in my life. Because, you see, the reality of my actions all of a sudden hit me like a ton of bricks.

Every morning I'd wake up and the first thing on my mind was Jessica. The Bible tells us sometimes we don't have words and we just groan because there are things going on too deep in our hearts that we can't really express. I'd lay on my bed and I could only pray one prayer, and could only say one thing. I would just groan: **"Oh, God! Jessica!"** Because I never in my life imagined that I could hurt one of my children the way I had hurt her. How in the world could I have done this? I still don't have an answer. Just living with the fact that I'd walked off and left her was more than I could bear.

And so, I waited. It took Jessica about three weeks to deal with me showing up and to overcome her fears and to allow the Lord to begin to deal in her heart.

Jessica:

When I thought about any daddy things, when I had any daddy needs, when I had any daddy dreams for my whole life, they went in this box. It was this pretty little black box in my heart, with a 1980s style huge bright pink bow on it. Now, I was in this position and I had to deal with what was in that box.

For three weeks I was silent and Dad/Jimmie heard nothing from me. I didn't respond or reply. For those three weeks I grieved. I now had to be something else, someone else than what I'd been. You see, for almost 39 years I was fatherless. I was abandoned. I was orphaned in a way. Every time there was a daddy/daughter date night or a father/daughter dance, or something daddies should have been there for, he wasn't. There was Grandpa…sometimes. But there wasn't Dad.

Now, I had to look all of this in the face and address it… and what in the world do I do with that!? So, I wrestled. I wrestled with God because what God said is, *"Give it to me."* And what I said was, "No! I have the right. I am justified. I can be whatever I want and I want to be angry and I want to be bitter. I want to be mad because he wasn't there for anything…ever! And NOW he wants to be my daddy?! Are you kidding me!?"

And God said, *"No. You don't get to have that."*

Chapter Ten

**Note: The words that you are about to read are the actual words that were used in our journey. These are some of the most sacred words that we've ever shared with each other. They include many heroes, my wife Sherri and our children, Jason, Amanda, and a host of other people who helped us on our journey.

As you read this, I hope you will open your heart and allow the words that were spoken to bring healing and peace to every part of your life.

–Jimmie

Jimmie:

Early in March I was in Daytona—I wasn't watching the race—I was there for Bike Week playing concerts all week. I sent Jessica a brief email to touch base and let her know I was thinking of her:

March 7, 2011 at 8:13am
Subject: Have a Great Week
To: Jessica
From: Jimmie

I've been thinking and praying for you a lot. It's going to be a great week, enjoy it.

I'm hoping to hear from you soon.
Love, Jimmie

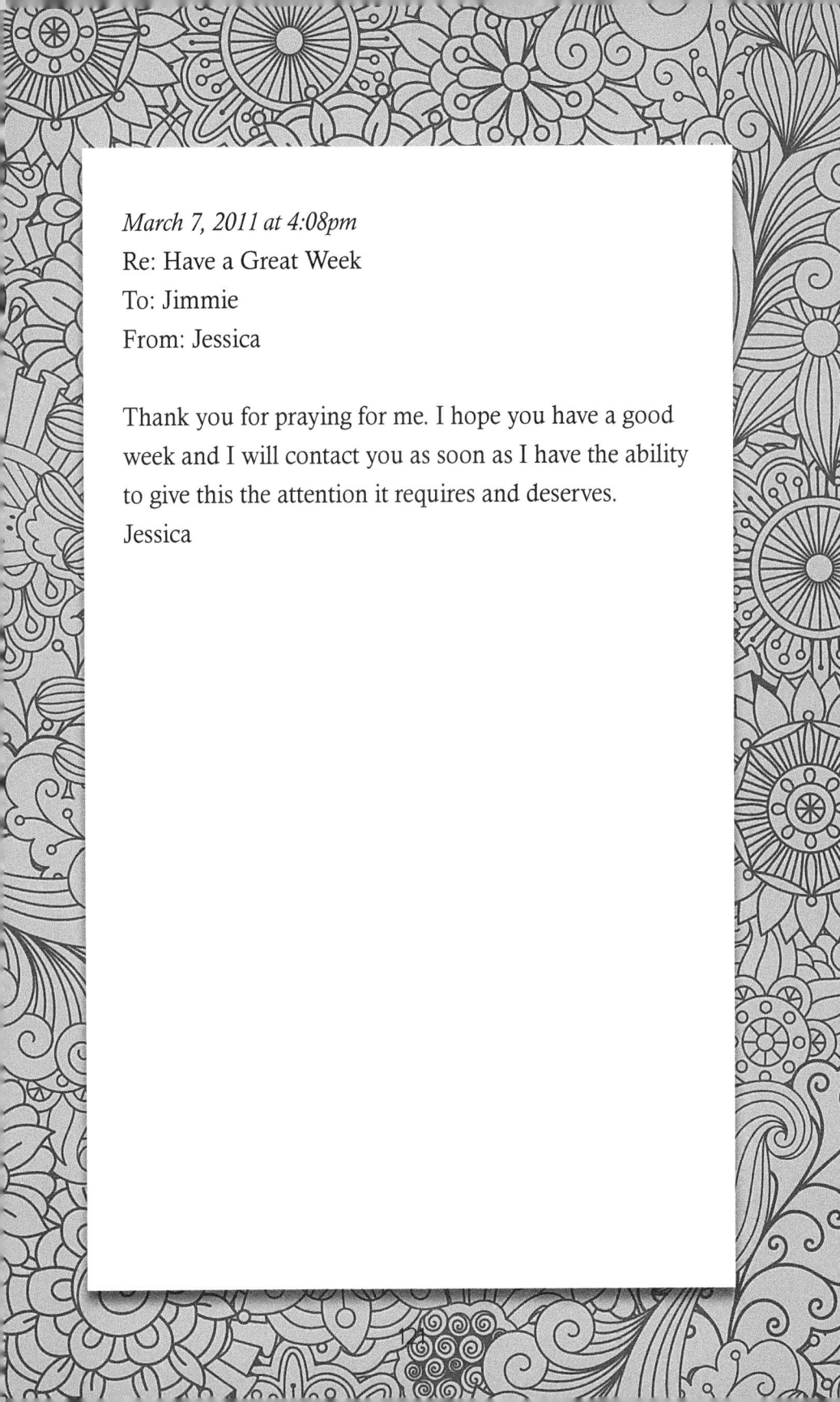

March 7, 2011 at 4:08pm
Re: Have a Great Week
To: Jimmie
From: Jessica

Thank you for praying for me. I hope you have a good week and I will contact you as soon as I have the ability to give this the attention it requires and deserves.
Jessica

On March 8, the following day, I sent another email to Jessica

March 8, 2011 at 5:22am
Subject: My Prayers For You
To: Jessica
From: Jimmie

Since February 13, my heart and mind has been full of one thought: "you." When I wake up the first words out of my mouth are "Oh God! Jessica." It comes from the very deepest part of me I don't remember ever praying a prayer that is this deep and important. I know that Jesus hears it. I pray and wait for you.

Love,
Jimmie

And Jessica responded:
Tuesday, March 8, 2011 at 5:30 PM
RE: Subject: My Prayers For You
To: Jimmie
From: Jessica

Jimmie,

Thank you for the messages. I'm sorry I haven't responded before now. I hope you can understand this isn't easy for me. For nearly 39 years you really didn't exist. You were a name that I only heard whispers of. I heard enough of these whispers to know you play guitar and had curly hair. But Mom never talked about you and I was content not to ask.

Years ago, I dealt with my emotions surrounding your absence and packed them up in a pretty little box in my heart. Now, after living my life not knowing of my father, the little girl in me wants to run to you, arms wide open. However, the woman in me wants to ask where you've been and why now.

Now I have to wipe off the dust and look at it all again. For a very long time I was hurt and felt rejected and unwanted. At other times I was incredibly angry that there would not be a father to see me dance, watch as I graduated or to give me away when I got married. After so long, you're here and it's hard. Not unwelcome, or unwanted, but very hard.

I would, at some point, like to meet you on my terms.

I would like to know if your family knows about me? It's important that they know about me. I have taken the time to look at both your Facebook page and your website. The availability of all that information has helped me in processing all this. For now, I would like to get to know more about you and your family before moving to a point where we may meet. I hope you understand that. This is very hard for me, but thanks for showing up.

Jessica

P.S. This is a picture of LeRoy and I the day he left for Afghanistan. (May 2010)

Jimmie:

And when she wrote those words, "Thanks for showin' up" I knew God was speaking to my family. Because when people ask Sherri and me to describe what we do, we always tell them that we have the "ministry of showin' up." The equation is: Christ in us and where we go, He goes, and where He goes, stuff happens. When she wrote those words, I knew that there was something happening here that was very, very wonderful.

We went back to the house we were staying in at Daytona; it was a house of an old biker dude. It was a nice house, but had no furniture, so all we had was an air mattress. I took the next five hours to draft an email to answer her questions. It was the most important and significant email I had ever written. I wanted to be sure I was honest. I wanted to be sure my words were directed by the Lord.

Tuesday, March 8, 2011 at 11:22 PM
To: Jessica
From Jimmie

Jessica,

Okay here goes. I pray I get this right! It is the most important email I've ever written. I know this is hard for you and the last thing in the world I want is to make it harder.

First, I am sorry for not being there for you. It is the biggest mistake of my life. And I mean that. I will ask this and when you're ready you can grant it if you want. Please forgive me. I am sorry for all the days that I've missed and all the pain that I've caused you. You have every right to be angry with me. I understand that. When you can find it in your heart, please forgive me.

As I write this, it is hard for me to write as I don't want anything I write to come across as an excuse--there is no acceptable excuse for my actions concerning you from 1972 until February 13, 2011. So, if it reads like an excuse, know it is not what I mean.
Okay? I also don't want this to sound like I am blaming your mother. I am not. I take complete responsibility for

my actions. What has happened is my fault alone and no one is to blame but me.

Your Questions:

Where have I been?

Living a life of "bad assumptions" that brought me to February 13.

In the fall 1971 I was 17 and was a drug crazed, selfish, undisciplined kid. I had dropped out of school and was wasting my life and hurting everyone I loved. I was dating your mother off and on nothing serious as far as I was concerned. We were having fun taking drugs and both making very bad choices. One evening your mother told me she was pregnant and I didn't believe her. I don't remember ever speaking to or hearing anything from your mother from that night till February 13. My "bad assumption" was I assumed I was right. Either she wasn't pregnant or that I was not the father. She didn't contact me and I didn't contact her. I heard later that she was pregnant and that she had a little girl. I guess your mother assumed I didn't want to be there and she was right when I was 17. I would have only hurt you like I was hurting everyone.

I lived under that bad assumption until one day I saw you and your Grandfather at Waid's in Liberty. I saw you and I knew you were mine. You were so beautiful. I wanted so badly to go to you but I again assumed that I wasn't wanted or needed in your life. I assumed your mother didn't want me to be involved and I can't speak for her, but I think she thought I didn't want to be involved. Looking back at that time I should have been a bigger man than I was and got involved but I didn't. So, I continued living in my bad assumptions.

Why now?

Simple. Because I was invited.

I found your uncle Randy's Facebook page about a year ago and found your mother. I sent her a friend request hoping she would invite me into your world. And that is what happened February 13. I got the most wonderful email I have ever received, "I think it's overdue for you to meet your daughter and grandsons"! I had not even heard your name before that day. I would have been on the first flight I could have found on February 13th and came straight to you but I knew this is on your terms not mine.

Does my family know?

My wife Sherri knows. I have not told your brother Jason or your sister Amanda yet. I am excited to tell Jason & Amanda about you. They are great people, love Jesus, you will like them a lot and I know they will love you. I wanted to wait and see how you wanted to proceed before I told them. I told Sherri many years ago. We have talked much about you since 2/13 and in her words "our hearts and our home are open to you." Sherri is a great woman, I know you will like her. I am traveling on the east coast for the next week. As soon as I return home I will speak with them. Look them up on Facebook Jason Bratcher & Amanda Bratcher Truxal. Amanda has two kids, Mikaela is 9 and Zayne is 7.

I met Sherri in 1973 at a Black Sabbath concert, she got pregnant and six months into her pregnancy we got married. We call it the marriage made in hell. It was terrible, very abusive and violent.

It lasted not quite 3 years and we divorced. I was on my course of hurting everyone in my life. I was out of control and heading straight toward death. My sister Patsy started attending church giving her life to Jesus and she and others started praying for me & Sherri.

About a year later on December 19, 1976 Sherri, Jason and I stumbled into a little country church in NW MO with a marriage license. We had to hide from our parents and friends, they would have locked us up rather than see us get back together. The only way the pastor would marry us was if I would give my life to Jesus. I agreed, thinking it didn't mean anything. Little did I know but Jesus invaded my heart that night and forgave me and changed me. From that moment till now I have given my life to following and serving Jesus as best as I can. Amanda was born 10 months later. Jason is divorced and living in KC. Amanda lives in Weston, MO and has been my personal assistant for the last 9 years.

That brings me to my biggest question for myself. Why after getting right with God and being forgiven didn't I come back and get you? I am extremely disappointed in myself And I don't know if I'll get past that disappointment ever. I said it before and I'll say it again I'm sorry, forgive me.

So, here I am now and I can't do anything about the past. I hope we can at some point move beyond it. Whenever you're ready.

I don't know anything about you or your life. Except you have my eyes? I think you may have my hair? I hope you didn't get the world-famous Bratcher nose? If you did I'm really sorry about that. Sherri kicked me in the face one night when we were fighting (our first marriage) and I had my nose rebuilt and got a little of that Bratcher nose removed. I don't know anything about your boys. Right now, my only focus is you. You tell me about those guys when you want. Okay?

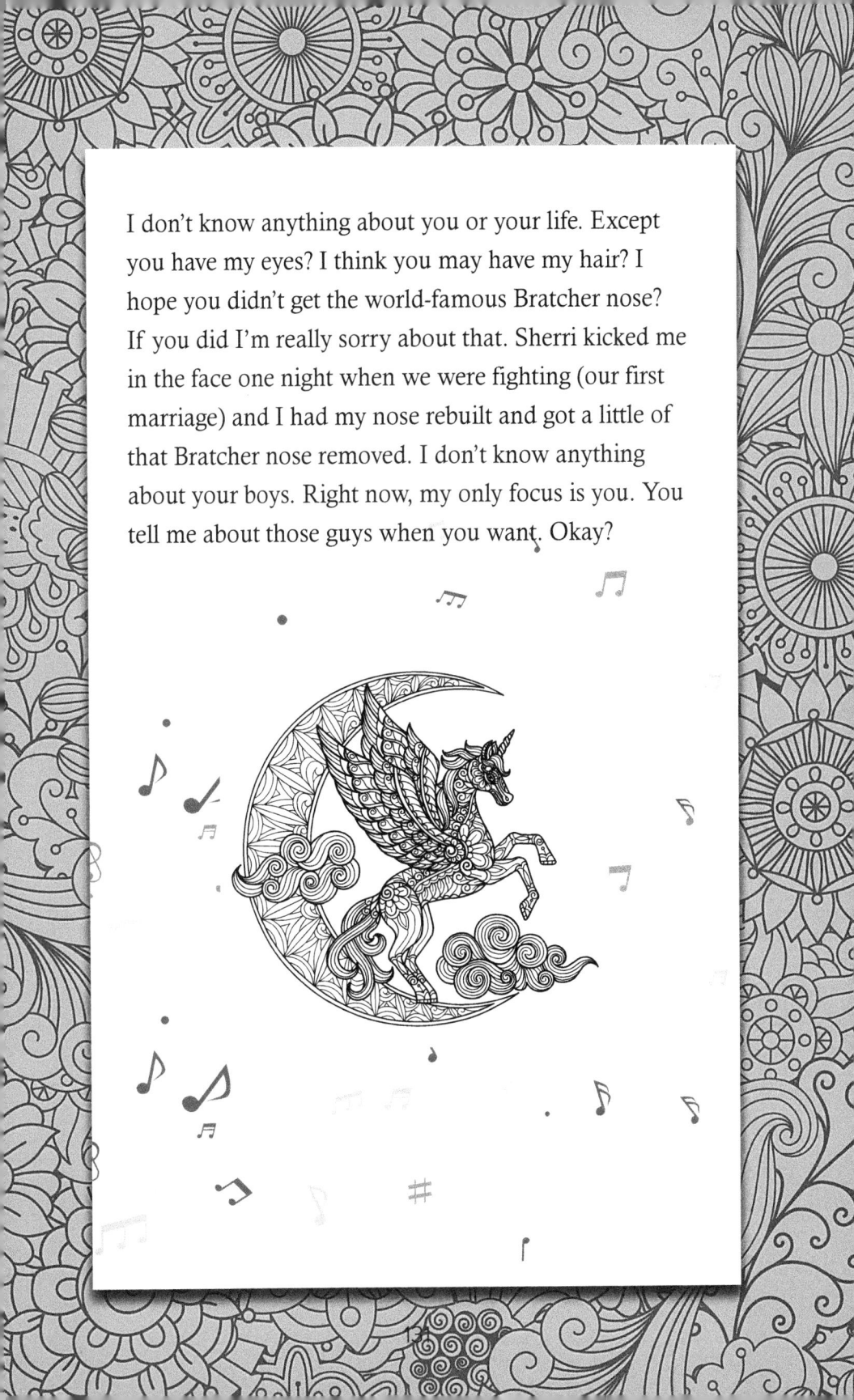

I wrote a song a few months ago, it is the opening track on my CD that is coming out in a couple of weeks. I thought the way I wrote the song was strange. It's about forgiveness but only the hope of forgiveness. Since 2/13 when I hear the song "It's a New Day" all I think about is you. I would like for you to hear it. I would attach it to this email but I only have my phone with me and no Internet where I am at. So, if you would go to http://www.jimmiebratcher.com/Exchange and click on the song "01 It's a New Day.mp3" and listen to it, it expresses how I feel about this moment.

Well I'm going to stop here. There is much more to tell you. Do you have more questions? If you do I'll do my best to answer them.

Jessica, I hope the little girl wins! Because know this, if your heart has room for me in it, I'm coming with my arms open wide. I've never heard your voice. I've never seen you smile. I've never felt your touch. If you'll let me in I'll never leave you again. I am a Father waiting for his first-born child to arrive. Goodnight!

Much Love,
Jimmie

Chapter Eleven

Constant Communication

Jimmie:

We started a flurry of messages back and forth. I've kept and cherished all of them. Writing back and forth was like a full-time job. Communicating with each other was all we could do.

Day Two:

Wednesday, March 9, 2011 at 7:56 AM
To: Jimmie
From: Jessica

Thank you for your honesty and openness. I appreciate your willingness to "throw it all out there." That takes courage that is built on a life of "bad assumptions." So, here's some of my story.

Growing up, we were in and out of my grandparents' house. My mother made the best decisions she knew how. There was a lot of drugs, alcohol and abuse around for years. When I was 13, Jim and I went to live with my grandparents and my sister and brother went to live with their dad. Mom was going through another divorce and couldn't handle the teenagers. The conversation she and I had is as clear as day.

She was sending my brother to live with my grandparents because she couldn't control him and his path was potentially very deadly. With a tearstained face told me she had no one to send me to. At that moment, I made my first really smart and self-preserving decision. I went to my grandparents.

After that I flirted with stupidity and drugs. But managed to graduate in the top 3% of my class. My brother Jim was very protective of me and I'm still very thankful for how he prevented me from doing a lot of harm to myself. At 19 I decided I didn't like my grandparents' rules anymore and spent a year wandering around going from couch to couch and fortunately was under God's protection even though I didn't know Him. I was never hurt or abused, just neglected and unloved. In the fall of 1992, I found myself about to lose my place to live, jobless and alone in Tucson. I walked into the recruiter's office. And left for boot camp 3 weeks later.

I was an Arabic Linguist in the Air Force for 10 years or as LeRoy says "the paramilitary branch of the post office." During that time, I married and divorced, had my son Aaron. My mother came to live with me just before I got married. I divorced Rick for nothing important. At that time in my life I was too hot headed and passionate and he was very lukewarm, not a good combination. In the fall of 1997 I met LeRoy. I knew the day I met him I knew we would grow old together.

Simply put, (according to him) he is awesome and very tolerant of my ways! LeRoy and I were married in 1999 in Cambridge, England. In 2000, our son Jacob was born. In 2001 we gained custody of Matt and Seth (LeRoy's boys from his first marriage). LeRoy was set to get promoted, we couldn't get assigned together. So I left the Air Force and started working for the Dept. of Defense. I've been there since then.

About 3 and a half years ago, I walked into a Christmas Eve service and saw a girl I served with in the Air Force who was more of a mess than me and at that point, God turned my life down a different path. I've been a believer since then. I'm blessed to serve on the women's ministry leadership team and I am learning to live as God called me.

We're a busy family. LeRoy retired from the Marine Corps in 2006 and we both work for DOD now. Our oldest son Matt attends college and is a very gifted athlete, Seth has chosen the life of a mechanic/redneck and enjoys it very much, Aaron is a gifted musician who loves to play the guitar and is a 10th grader "I know more than YOU" type, and Jacob is just finishing elementary school and according to LeRoy, is the only "cool" one left! It is important to me that you understand Matt and Seth are just as much my kids as if I had given birth to them myself. We are a very close family. We're a lot loud and definitely not formal or snooty. We're very much jeans and t-shirts but can pull off tuxedos if we have to.

Thank you again for being so honest and open with me.

I look forward to hearing more from you.

Wednesday, March 9, 2011 at 9:06 AM
To: Jessica
From: Jimmie

Jessica,

Thanks so much for sharing your story. I am traveling today and I will spend what time I have between stops writing more to you. I read your email to Sherri weeping. Sorry, I'm a very emotional man. Sherri said this and I agree, "there has always been something missing in our lives and Jessica, LeRoy, and their boys are it."

Bless you much today
Love,
Jimmie

Wednesday, March 9, 2011 at 10:50 AM
To: Jimmie
From: Jessica

I'm pretty emotional too. That's why it took me so long to reply.

Where are you traveling to?

Wednesday, March 9, 2011 at 11:45 AM
To: Jessica
From: Jimmie

We are today in Orlando. The band and I have been doing some concerts at Daytona Bike Week with the 500,000 bikers that are there. We finished yesterday and the band flew home this morning. I am speaking tonight at a church in Eustis, FL, near here. Then I am speaking Sunday in North Augusta, SC. Then either heading home Monday, or only if you want, coming to see you if that is what your terms tell me to do, no pressure.

As far as emotions are concerned, I've been completely wiped out since 2/13. My band thinks something is terribly wrong with me. I had to set them down last night and tell them that I'm just seeing a miracle in the making and I will tell them something wonderful soon. My drummer Dave is separated from his wife and lives with your brother Jason. So, I don't want to tell Dave till I tell Jase.

I've been just breaking out in waves of joy and tears. Again, coming from a very, very deep place inside of me. I tried to eat this morning and could only sit at Cracker Barrel and weep.

I want you to know you are loved, you are accepted as part of me and my family. You are greatly valued beyond any worth. You will be safe in my love. I'll give my all, my very best to never hurt you.

I am working on some family history for you next.

Love you,
Jimmie

Wednesday, March 9, 2011 at 1:33 PM
To: Jimmie
From: Jessica

You seem to do a lot with Bikers. I noticed on your website you've been to Sturgis recently. I've always wanted a bike, but my daredevil husband doesn't think it's a good idea living so close to DC with all the crazy drivers. I have to say I'd like to ride in Rolling Thunder just once... just to say I did.

Emotionally... the roller coaster has been incredible and indescribable. Initially I really couldn't keep it together. I took a couple of days off work just to regroup. Since Feb 13th, LeRoy started working in Charlottesville, VA during the week and coming home on the weekends. Last weekend I had the women's ministry team retreat. I've had such a ride that I was barely functioning. Mostly I have been going through motions, just getting my head around it.

If you and Sherri are willing to detour slightly, I do really want to meet you. Head up to Charlottesville VA on Monday and have dinner with LeRoy and me.

Thank you also for the family history. Do your sisters know about me? Mom told me Di, Randy and Ron don't know. I'm not sure my grandparents do either.

The adventure is only beginning. :)

Wednesday, March 9, 2011 at 1:59 PM
To: Jessica
From: Jimmie

Jessica,

You've made me very happy. MONDAY!!!
My sisters do not know yet, I will let them know when I get home or as soon as I tell the kids.

Monday!!! I get to meet my girl. We will gladly be there. If you can give me a restaurant or what part of town that would help. I'm buying anything you want. Pick some place really nice. But not too formal. Pick your favorite.

You should have a bike. Well, I'll let LeRoy jump in on that one. I don't even have one at the moment. If you don't get one I will find one and come and take you to Rolling Thunder. When is it?

I will leave it up to you to tell your mother we are talking, if that's okay? It's not that I mind, I'm just not sure how to handle that. I'll do whatever you would like.

I Love You, Jimmie

Day Three

Thursday, March 10, 2011 at 6:40 AM
Subject: Good Morning Jessica
To: Jessica
From: Jimmie

I missed not telling you goodnight, SO Good morning.... you're BEAUTIFUL....

We had a good evening at Family Bible Church in Eustis, FL. It is a very happy church. The people there laughed a lot and liked all my jokes. I wasn't trying to tell jokes, I was just really funny for some reason. I was just happy because I made it through the night without breaking into tears, thinking about you.

We are staying with our friends Ron & Sandy, they pastor a church here in Longwood, FL. You would like them, they are wonderful loving people. We told them about you at dinner last night. Well, so much for dinner. We all wept, prayed and thanked God for you being sent to us. You have a wonderful day.

Thursday, Mar 10, 2011 at 7:55 AM
Re: Good Morning Jessica
To: Jimmie
From: Jessica

I'm happy you didn't cry so much. LeRoy and I were just laughing. I'm very much an all or nothing kind of person. It's very obvious to me I get that and being emotional from you. It's nice to know where some of my quirks come from.

I spent some time looking at restaurants last night. I'm so emotional I'm having trouble focusing. :-) I'll have something in the next day or so.

Have a great day.
Jessica

Thursday, March 10, 2011 at 8:11 AM
Re:Re Good Morning Jessica
To: Jessica,
From: Jimmie

Yea, I bet I can tell you some stories about you and why you act the way you do. That is going to be fun discovery. We've got a lot to laugh about. I look forward to hearing you laugh and seeing you smile.

I'll find some place for us to have dinner. I've got some time in the next couple of days and I am the king of logistics. What is your favorite food?

You are one blessed girl,
Jimmie

Thursday, March 10, 2011 at 8:23 AM
To: Jimmie
From: Jessica

A friend of mine just recommended Duners. Said it's a bit pricey but has an exceptional atmosphere. I love food. It can be a greasy spoon or 5 star. I don't mind so long as it's good. :-)

Thursday, March 10, 2011 at 9:59 AM
Subject: Jason & Amanda
To: Jessica
From: Jimmie

I felt like I needed to call and tell Jason & Amanda, so I did. Amanda has access to my email account and I didn't want to chance her reading something between us and not understand.

They are both extremely excited!!! I sent them your email address and Facebook page so you may be hearing from them soon.

They are excited to meet you and welcome you into YOUR family.

Oh, and Amanda has already told her husband Jonathan before I could call him. That should tell you how excited she is.

Welcome Home,
Jimmie

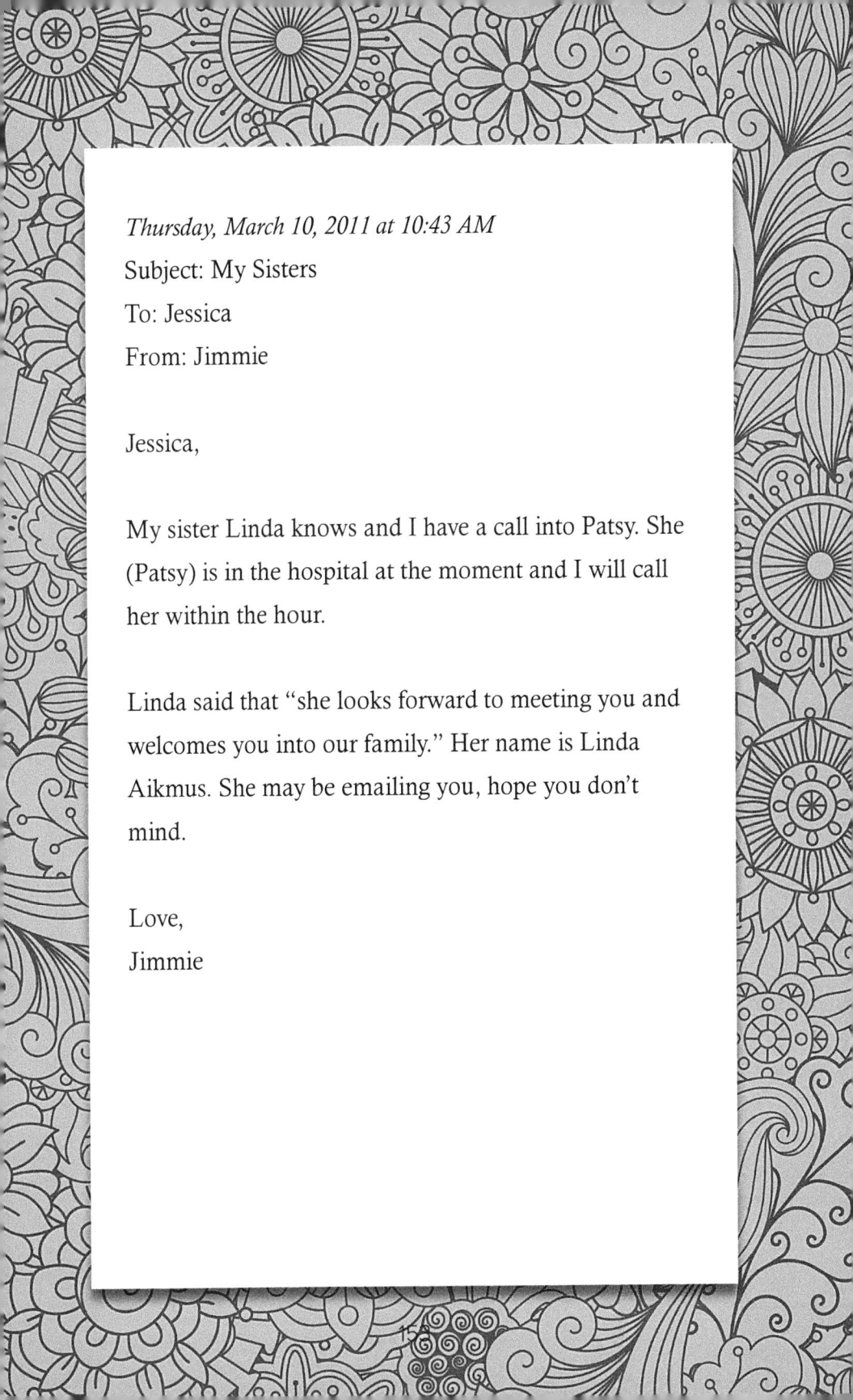

Thursday, March 10, 2011 at 10:43 AM
Subject: My Sisters
To: Jessica
From: Jimmie

Jessica,

My sister Linda knows and I have a call into Patsy. She (Patsy) is in the hospital at the moment and I will call her within the hour.

Linda said that "she looks forward to meeting you and welcomes you into our family." Her name is Linda Aikmus. She may be emailing you, hope you don't mind.

Love,
Jimmie

Thursday, March 10, 2011 at 11:10 AM
Re: Jason & Amanda
To: Jimmie
From: Jessica

Amanda has already emailed me. I'll keep an eye out for one from Linda. Why is Patsy in the hospital? What can I pray for her?

Thursday, March 10, 2011 at 11:19 AM
To: Jessica
From: Jimmie

Jessica,

Cool, Amanda was really excited.... and Jason too. But Amanda is off the charts about you.

Patsy has some infections in her stomach or something, I am calling her now.

Just so you'll know YOU MAKE ME HAPPY!!!! I am really, really HAPPY....Jimmie

Thursday, Mar 10, 2011 at 11:32 AM
To: Jimmie
From: Jessica

I'm happy too.

From Amanda to Jimmie

Thursday, March 10, 2011 at 12:38 PM
Re: My New Sister Jessica
From: Amanda
To: Jimmie

Hey, I just want to let you know that Jessica responded to my email. She seems super nice! She said she is overwhelmed by the warm reception. I wanted to let you know that this doesn't make me think any less of you! You are a great dad! I know you are struggling with this right now, but you are THE BEST! and don't ever doubt that about yourself.

I love ya!
Amanda

Thursday, March 10, 2011 at 6:46 PM

Subject: What is Forgiveness

To: Jimmie

From: Jessica

I got this from my Jennifer, my other sister today... wow. "Forgiveness is giving up the hope that the past could have been different."

Thursday, March 10, 2011 at 7:51 PM
Re: What is Forgiveness
To: Jessica
From: Jimmie

WOW!!! Is right. I'm trying to get my head around that now. That is a very remarkable truth. I know that God really, really loves you. You are one very precious, special and remarkable woman.

I know the past is powerful. I am struggling with it as I know you are but in a different way. I only know the future is MORE POWERFUL and full of great things for you and me. Things like hope, love and peace. Those things that only Jesus can give us.

Let's discover that future together.

I love you,
Jimmie

Jimmie:

I knew that there was something so powerful and so sacred about to take place. That it was beyond all that I could ask or think. It was one of those moments that eyes have not seen and ears have not heard. The things that were possible, the things that God had prepared for us, had never really entered into my heart...yet, He was doing more than I could ever ask or imagine.

Jessica:

Now at this point I had started to tell people. Only people who were close to us. And the stories that started coming out of the woodwork were horrific. Stories of people who have tried to reconcile with their families or a parent, or as a parent to a child and how disastrous it had been. I had one tell me: *Don't tell him where you live. Don't let him meet your kids. Don't show him any pictures because I had to get a restraining order against my dad because he stole my identity after we met.* These were the constant conversations. Every one of them! Everything that was happening at that point was contrary to God's saying: *Trust me.*

Everything that could possibly hit me to pull me away and say: *No, I'm not going to do this*, constantly bombarded me. But I wasn't willing to give it up. I just knew that this was something that God had for us, so I pushed through the fear.

Day Five

Saturday, March 12, 2011 at 6:05 AM
Subject: Good morning
To: Jimmie
From: Jessica

I was up early (I'm always up early). Thinking about you. I know you've been a pastor for most of your adult life. I know that you know Jesus. God put a few things on my heart this morning in the form of scriptures. If I'm being presumptuous or anything else please tell me. I hear blunt pretty well and you won't hurt my feelings.

As I'm reading my devotionals and hanging out with God in the quiet predawn hours, I hear over and over again. Don't worry. Be at peace. Be open to what I tell you and it's going to be fine. Trust me and rely on me and I'll see you through whatever is next.

God let this happen at this time in our lives for a reason. I look back at the last 4o years and I couldn't have received you except as a small child. You weren't in a good place then and God had plans for you too. At this time in my life I rely on God, where I have always relied on the world. I relied on my understanding and the world's answers. I don't pretend to know what theology you follow or any particulars, but I know this: God is telling me over and over again to relax, trust Him and rely on His understanding, not mine. I'm really feeling that's just as much for you too.

I don't have any animosity, I'm not angry. I know there are times when you could have been here and you weren't. We can't change that. I know that you're here now and I'm very excited about getting to know you and MY family.

God has put you up against some greater challenges than this one. Don't worry. It's going to be GREAT. :)

Saturday, March 12, 2011 at 6:46 AM
Re: Good morning
To: Jessica
From: Jimmie

Good morning sweetheart.

Thank you, thank you, thank you, for the word from the Lord. You got me weeping right off the bat this morning. Weeping with the greatest joy a man could ever have. One of his own children comforting and understanding. I like blunt too, so bring it baby.... I want you to never hide your feelings with me. I know there will be times when you hurt, times when you rejoice and times when we both make mistakes. When you hurt it's okay, it's okay when we make mistakes, it will never change who you are and how I feel about you. You're my girl to bluntly put it.

There are just times with me and Sherri when we read your story about not having any place to go when you were a teenager that breaks us down. But you're right, God has a plan and it's NOT going to be alright... it IS alright, and I know that with every cell in my body.

We, ALL of us, are just fine, in fact we ARE now COMPLETE as a family with you finishing the masterpiece.

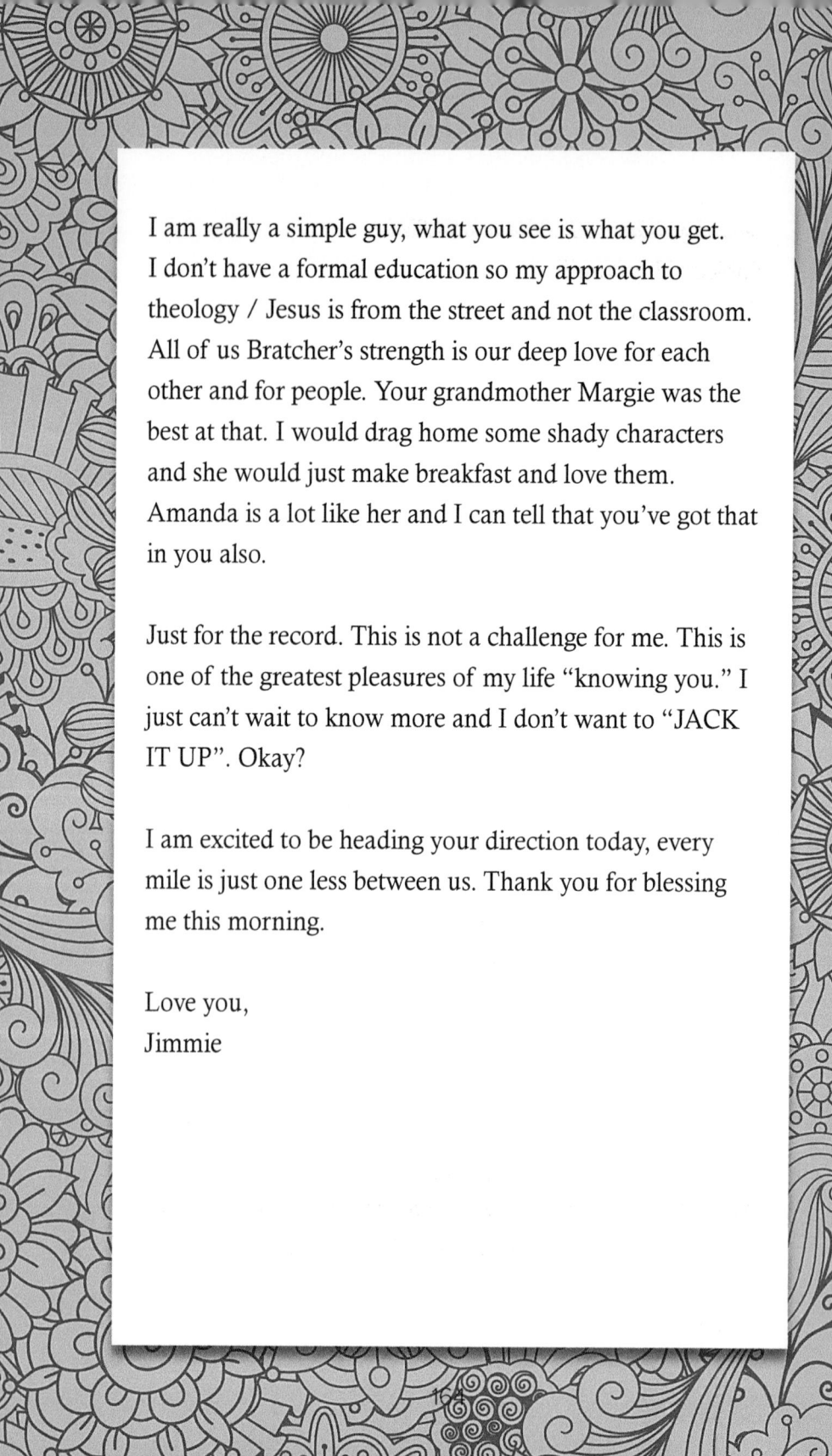

I am really a simple guy, what you see is what you get. I don't have a formal education so my approach to theology / Jesus is from the street and not the classroom. All of us Bratcher's strength is our deep love for each other and for people. Your grandmother Margie was the best at that. I would drag home some shady characters and she would just make breakfast and love them. Amanda is a lot like her and I can tell that you've got that in you also.

Just for the record. This is not a challenge for me. This is one of the greatest pleasures of my life "knowing you." I just can't wait to know more and I don't want to "JACK IT UP". Okay?

I am excited to be heading your direction today, every mile is just one less between us. Thank you for blessing me this morning.

Love you,
Jimmie

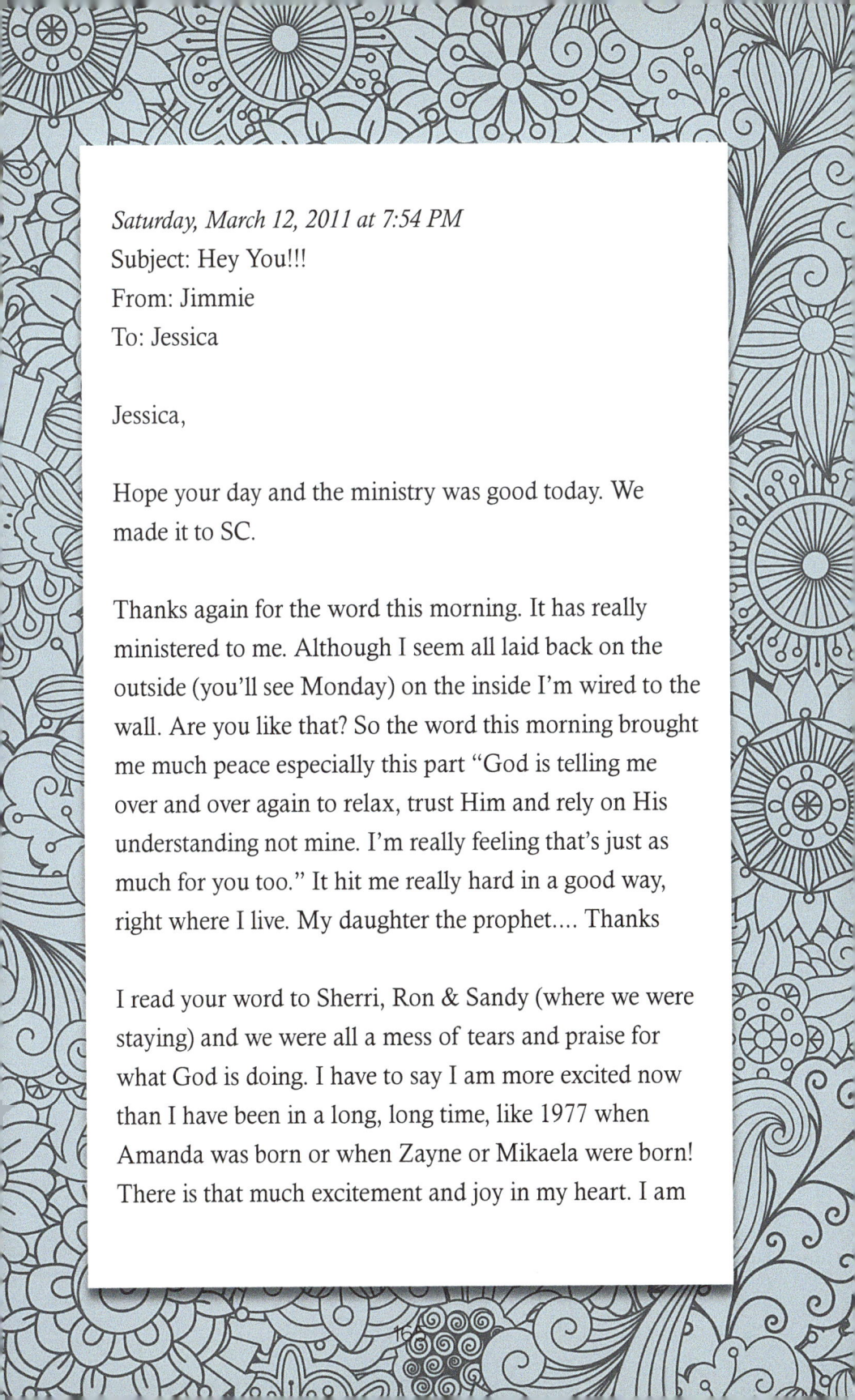

Saturday, March 12, 2011 at 7:54 PM
Subject: Hey You!!!
From: Jimmie
To: Jessica

Jessica,

Hope your day and the ministry was good today. We made it to SC.

Thanks again for the word this morning. It has really ministered to me. Although I seem all laid back on the outside (you'll see Monday) on the inside I'm wired to the wall. Are you like that? So the word this morning brought me much peace especially this part "God is telling me over and over again to relax, trust Him and rely on His understanding not mine. I'm really feeling that's just as much for you too." It hit me really hard in a good way, right where I live. My daughter the prophet.... Thanks

I read your word to Sherri, Ron & Sandy (where we were staying) and we were all a mess of tears and praise for what God is doing. I have to say I am more excited now than I have been in a long, long time, like 1977 when Amanda was born or when Zayne or Mikaela were born! There is that much excitement and joy in my heart. I am a basket case.... But WOW!!!! I think you or LeRoy can only imagine what it is like to welcome a daughter into the world. But I know!!! Sons are awesome but daughters are really, really special. I am glad that I've had this last week to write to you. It has made me SO thankful for my family who are all incredible and now for you. In my wildest dreams I could not have dreamed something this wonderful happening to me. And I am a dreamer, shoot I even wrote a book about dreams and still I could not have dreamed something this wonderful happening to me. Jessica you're a dream come true.

Thanks for being you, that is all I will ever expect from you. Just be yourself and nothing else and I will always be pleased.

Take care of the boys, email only if you have time. Tell LeRoy he's awesome.... in a Viking kind of way.... I'll explain later.

Love you, Jimmie

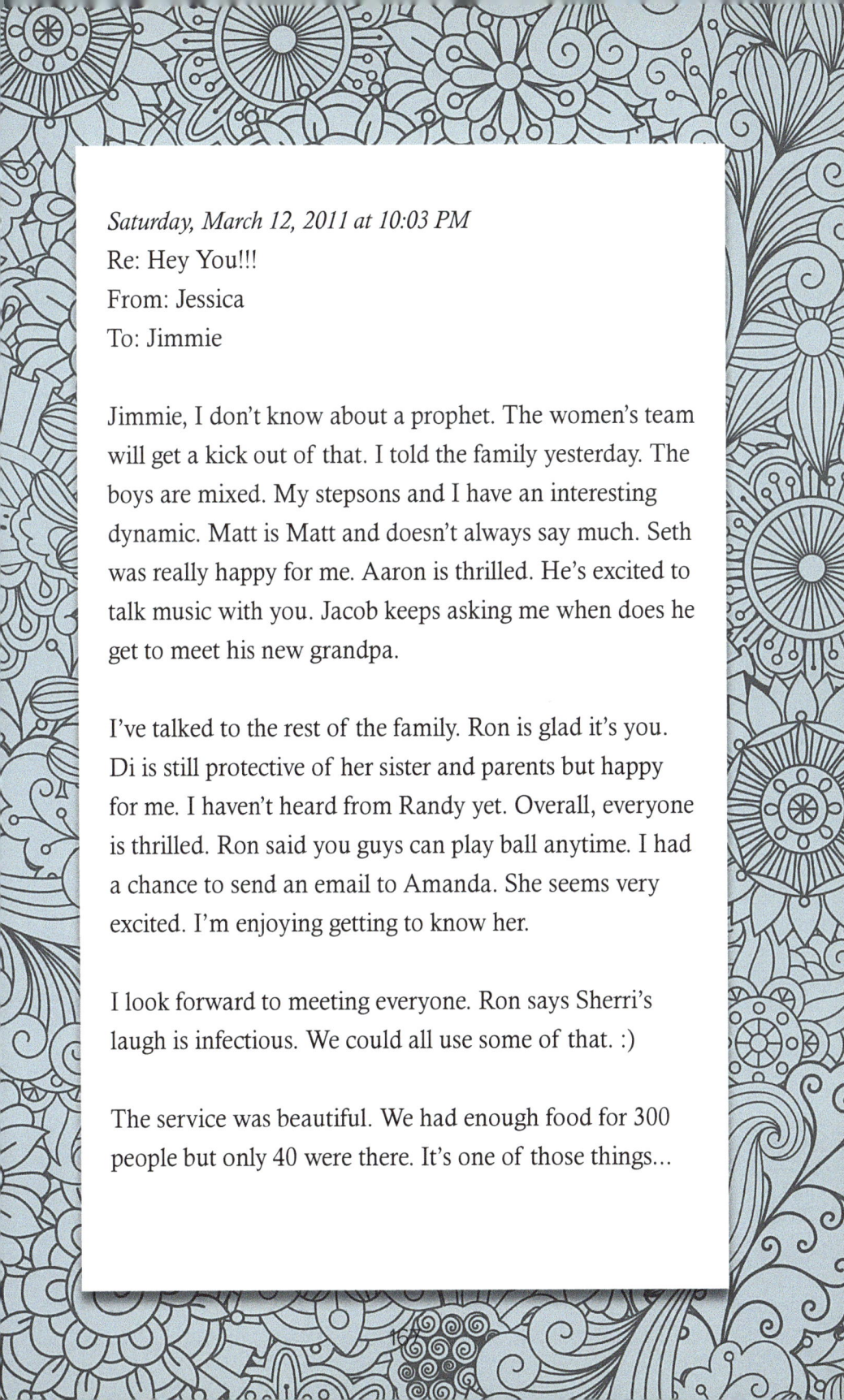

Saturday, March 12, 2011 at 10:03 PM
Re: Hey You!!!
From: Jessica
To: Jimmie

Jimmie, I don't know about a prophet. The women's team will get a kick out of that. I told the family yesterday. The boys are mixed. My stepsons and I have an interesting dynamic. Matt is Matt and doesn't always say much. Seth was really happy for me. Aaron is thrilled. He's excited to talk music with you. Jacob keeps asking me when does he get to meet his new grandpa.

I've talked to the rest of the family. Ron is glad it's you. Di is still protective of her sister and parents but happy for me. I haven't heard from Randy yet. Overall, everyone is thrilled. Ron said you guys can play ball anytime. I had a chance to send an email to Amanda. She seems very excited. I'm enjoying getting to know her.

I look forward to meeting everyone. Ron says Sherri's laugh is infectious. We could all use some of that. :)

The service was beautiful. We had enough food for 300 people but only 40 were there. It's one of those things…

Don't ask 100 church ladies to cook for a funeral service without some control. HA HA HA.

Ok, it's bedtime for me.

Good night.

Day Six

Re: Hey You!!!
Sunday, March 13, 2011 at 6:48 AM
To: Jessica
From: Jimmie

Jessica,

ONE MORE DAY....

You must have had a very busy day, WOW.
How do you feel now that you've told the boys? You okay? Tell those boys I'm looking forward to meeting them all.

I couldn't tell in your email did you tell your grandparents or did your mother tell them and how did they do? I don't think your grandfather liked me very much; for all the right reasons. What a blessing that you still have them here.

Ron and I did play ball together, though I was around Randy more. One of his best friends, Mark Butler, and I were good friends and that was my connection to the Cottinghams. I was never around Di much as she was pretty much gone by the time I was around. I would see Randy throughout the years at Chubby's where he worked.

Just for the record, and I will be very strong about this, okay? I am very interested in how your mother does through all this. It is important to me that she not be threatened or left out. I feel this could be a time of deep healing and restoration in her life and WE are very interested in that. I will let you guide me and Sherri through that. We can talk about this later as you feel led.

Enjoy church this morning. I hope I can concentrate, I think I can. I have slept well the last couple of nights so that is good. I am speaking twice today and doing a mini concert tonight "solo". This is my first time at this church so that makes it easier for me.

One more day.... Sherri said this morning she is excited to get to tomorrow.... There are no words that describe how excited I am about getting this day over and seeing you tomorrow. Have a great day today and enjoy being with the family of God.

Love you much, Jimmie

PS. Not just Sherri's laugh is infectious, she is infectious. You will like her a lot I hope. She had a very rough past growing up and she loves very deeply. She feels about you like you feel about Matt & Seth, you are that much a part of her already.

Facebook Post from Jimmie
Sunday, March 13 at 4:53pm

I'm having one of these in my life right now! "Eye has not seen, nor ear heard, nor have entered into the heart of man the things which God has prepared for those who love Him."

Sunday, March 13, 2011 at 7:22 PM
Subject: How's Your Day Been?
To: Jessica
From: Jimmie

Hope you had a great day. I've been thinking about you and the boys.

Hope you got to have some YOU time today!!!

We are all done in SC!!!! It was just fine. I found some new passion or some old passion I had buried. Anyway, it was good.

Tomorrow I hear your voice. I am excited.

Love,
Jimmie

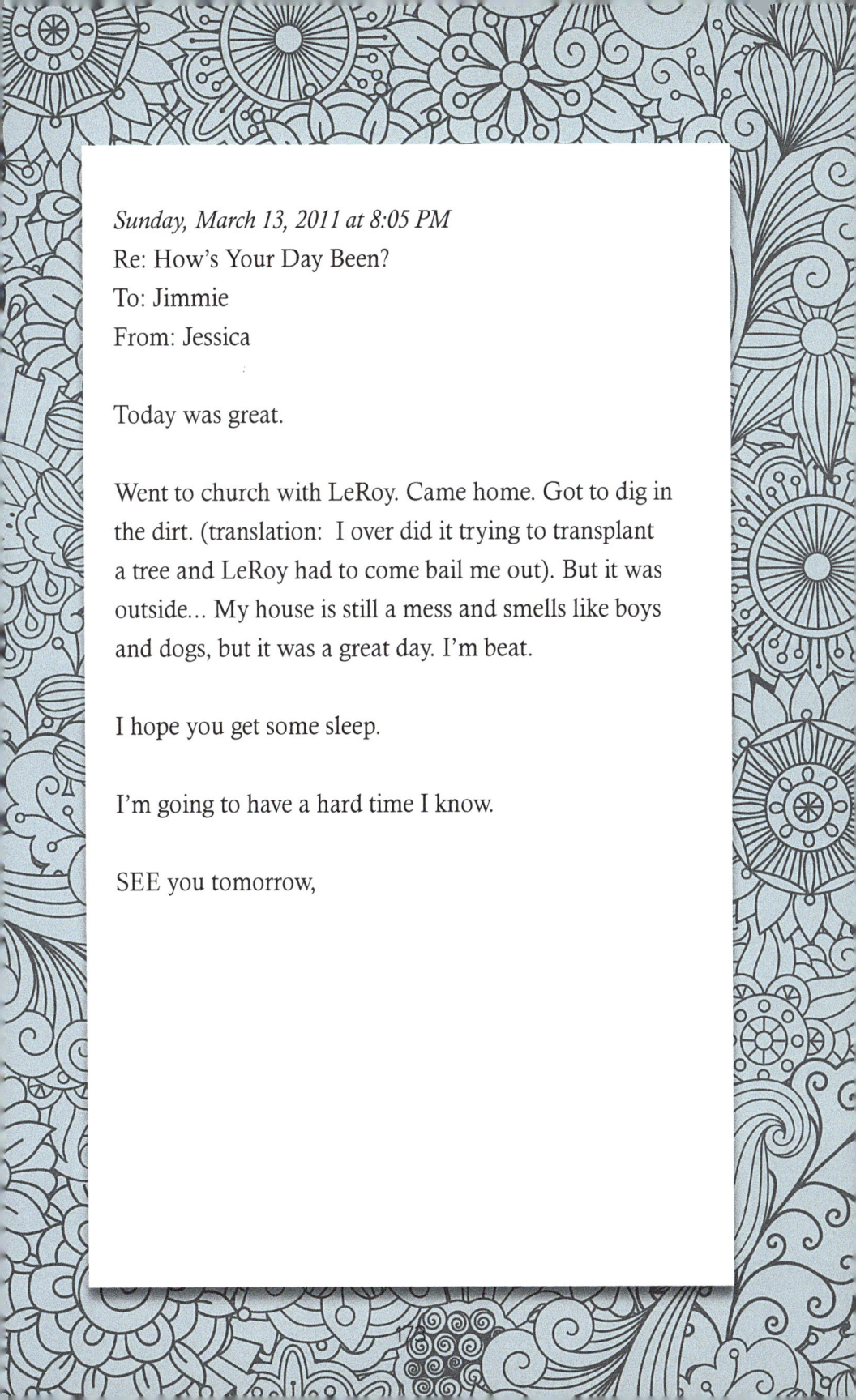

Sunday, March 13, 2011 at 8:05 PM
Re: How's Your Day Been?
To: Jimmie
From: Jessica

Today was great.

Went to church with LeRoy. Came home. Got to dig in the dirt. (translation: I over did it trying to transplant a tree and LeRoy had to come bail me out). But it was outside... My house is still a mess and smells like boys and dogs, but it was a great day. I'm beat.

I hope you get some sleep.

I'm going to have a hard time I know.

SEE you tomorrow,

Sunday, March 13, 2011 at 8:21 PM
Re: How's Your Day Been?
To: Jessica
From: Jimmie

Hey!!! I can dig it.

I won't sleep either I have a song about that called Restless for the Sun

Hey, what time tomorrow?

Love ya,
Jimmie

Facebook Post from Jimmie
Sunday, March 13 at 10:05pm
I hope I can sleep tonight? Miracles have a way of keeping you so excited that sleep is optional. What a wonderful miracle tomorrow will be.

Monday, March 14, 2011 at 1:32 AM
Ron Cottingham (Jessica's Uncle) commented on your status:

"Miracles are wonderful gifts. We celebrate with you."

Chapter Twelve

The Time Has Come

Day Seven

Monday, March 14, 2011 at 5:23 AM
Subject: Good Morning Today is The Day!!!
To: Jessica
From Jimmie

Jessica,

Well I'm up! What a great day to be alive. God is so good to us. In just a few hours we will meet. It's a dream come true. I am so excited. See you soon.

Love,
Jimmie

Facebook Post on Jimmie's Page
March 14, 2011 at 6:08 AM
I've got no words to properly express how I feel and just how GREAT God is to me and my family. No words will do so I'll just worship.

Monday, March 14, 2011 at 6:13 AM
Re: Good Morning Today is The Day!!!
To: Jimmie
From: Jessica

Good morning to you too. :) I've been at work for about an hour and I'm really having trouble concentrating already. I can see this is not going
to be a very productive day.
:)

Monday, March 14, 2011 at 6:23 AM
Re: Good Morning Today is The Day!!!
To: Jessica
From: Jimmie

Jessica,

You be at peace and remember the WORD you shared with me. "Relax, it's going to be fine". I am trying to live that word today. It's going to be fine.

Today I hear your voice, today I see your smile. A miracle!

I love you,
Jimmie

Monday, March 14, 2011 at 6:12 AM
Subject: In Case
To: Jessica
From: Jimmie

Just in case you need to communicate to us today, please DON'T call me. I only want to hear your voice for the first time in person and not on the phone. So text me if you need to contact us.

Soon....
Jimmie

Monday, March 14, 2011 at 7:46 AM
Subject: Jacob's bedtime prayers
To: Jimmie
From: Jessica

Last night as we're getting ready for bed. I poke my head in to see if Jacob wanted tucked in. He looks at me sheepishly and asks if I would help him say bedtime prayers. I asked what he wanted to pray about. He said, having a new grandpa. I tell him, "Just say: Dear God and whatever you're thinking. God will hear you and know exactly what you mean." He nodded, reassured.

So, picture me on my knees beside the bed. He's laying down, his hands folded and mine over his, his eyes closed but checking to make sure mine are closed too. He says, "Dear God. Thank you for bringing me a new grandpa who's a musician and a preacher. Thank you for Nana who helped get me my new grandpa. And thank you for all the other good things in my life."

Just thought you'd appreciate this.

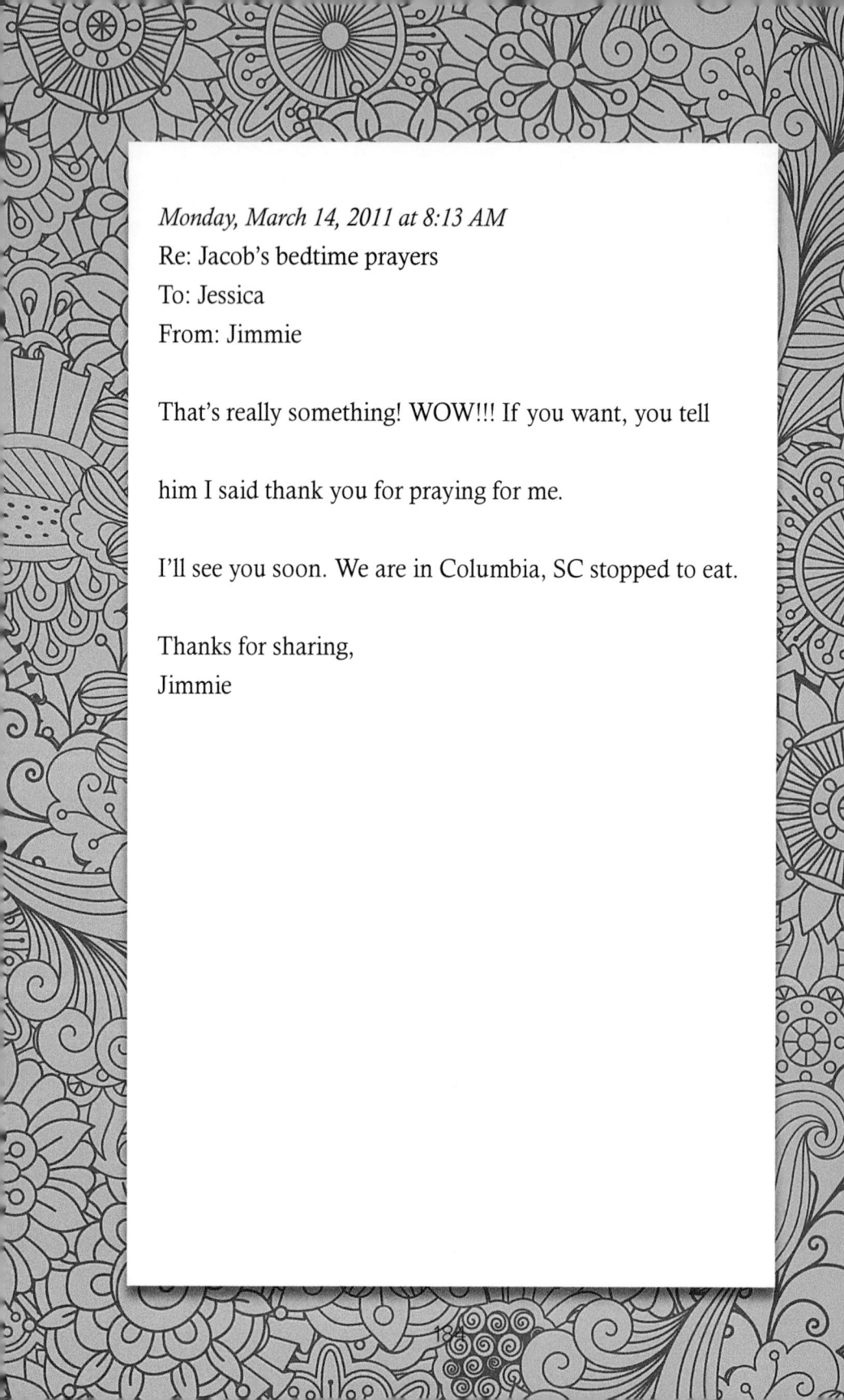

Monday, March 14, 2011 at 8:13 AM
Re: Jacob's bedtime prayers
To: Jessica
From: Jimmie

That's really something! WOW!!! If you want, you tell

him I said thank you for praying for me.

I'll see you soon. We are in Columbia, SC stopped to eat.

Thanks for sharing,
Jimmie

Monday, March 14, 2011 at 8:53 AM
To: Jimmie
From: Jessica

I'm still working, but heading out from here around noon in hopes of beating the traffic coming out of DC. We'll see if the boss has other plans. So far so good. :)

Jimmie:

And so, the time had come. We got to the restaurant and drove around the back of the parking lot when I saw two of the most beautiful people I had ever laid eyes on (I did just call LeRoy beautiful!!) standing behind the biggest pickup truck known to mankind. It belonged to LeRoy Strong: First Sergeant Retired Marine Corps Drill Instructor of the Year. And I figured he was packin'!! Sherri and I were in our legendary band van called The White Pearl. The White Pearl was lovingly known as a white trash treasure. We found a parking place and exited the van to stand face to face with my daughter for the very first time.

Jessica:

I was so anxious standing in the parking lot of the restaurant trying to figure out what I was going to do. I was terrified, but excited. It was like waiting for a Christmas present, but you don't know what's in the box. I had seen pictures of him and it was like looking in a mirror. I was so stressed out, so freaked out, so uneasy and in such unfamiliar territory. I had no idea what I was going to say or do. Despite all our communication, despite being all in, the whole time I kept going back to being justified in my anger and justified in all the reasons there could be to say "no" and hold him at arm's length. I wanted to give this man a piece of my mind. I longed to just scream at him and blast him, to lay nearly 40 years' worth of emotions on him. Oh, how I wanted to. I replayed those words over and over but there was something different this time. That box of all the daddy things I had locked away was open. God whispered to me: *No. You have to let it go. You've got to let me have all that. That is not my best for you. Your pain, your anger, your longing for justice are all less than what I promised.*

Then they drove around the corner in the biggest hippy van I've ever seen in my life! And in that moment when they got out, all those thoughts and emotions were replaced one by one with love, connection, hope, joy and the restoration began. The pain that had been taking up the room in my heart was gone. God took it away from me. He said: *You don't get to have it, but you get to have your daddy. For the first time in your life, he's here. I'm redeeming all the pain. I'm taking away all the hurt and I'm allowing you to know what the love of a father is, like only I can do."*

And right then, I remembered that prayer that I agonized over while with my dying father-in-law in hospice, when I cried, "So who's going to be my daddy now?!" and I knew that God was answering it, *"He is."*

Jimmie:

And, there she was. I couldn't believe it because she looked so much like me, it was like looking at my reflection… except she was so beautiful. There was no DNA test needed, it was so very obvious, that this is my daughter. I'd only seen her in pictures, had never seen her smile, or experienced the light shining from her eyes. I never felt her touch, her hug, the feel of her hand in mine. I'd made up my mind that I wasn't going to say the first word. I was going to be quiet until she spoke because I'd never heard her voice. You parents know how it is, how significant it is and how expectant you are to hear the first word that your child speaks. Well, I'd never had that opportunity with Jessica. I was so taken as I stood there looking at this beautiful young woman; I was so expectant of her first words. What would they be, what would they sound like? It was exactly as it was when Jason and Amanda were born, when I heard their voices for the very first time. It was a moment I will never forget, it was sacred, it was beautiful, it was perfect.

I tell people, I'm not the kind of person who uses "hi" or "hello" in a greeting, because I'm too cool for that. I'll say something like: "Hey…" with a cool jerk of the head, as if to say: yo or 'sup? Real cool like. It seemed like forever, but I know it was only for a moment until she spoke and for the first time I heard her voice. "Hey…" she said, with the same cool head jerk! From that very first moment genetics were speaking. "I'm a hugger." She threw her arms around me and we embraced. And we wept and we wept and stood holding each other for what seemed like forever, but was probably about 20 minutes.

We finally pulled ourselves together enough to go into what had to be the loudest restaurant in Virginia, and it was crowded, probably not the best choice of venues for carrying on conversation. We sat in the corner and tried to order and shared a little small talk over the noise and then, I said to Jessica, "We really don't want anything from you. We're not going to ask you for anything. It's not why we're here. I'm not going to even ask you for this, but sometime, I'm going to ask if you would forgive me."

Jessica:

As I reached across the table, I was aware that all of those negative emotions and wounds were gone. I took his hand in mine and replied with an honesty and truth I didn't know I possessed, "We can't change the past, but you're here now and we're cool." You see when I allowed God access to all those daddy things, I allowed the healing to begin. What had been transpiring over the previous three weeks for me, was real in that moment.

We talked and cried and were eating through the tears. At some point in the evening, amidst all of the conversation and Kleenex, Sherri gave me a gift. It was important to her to give me something that would be meaningful for this first meeting. I love meaningful gifts, and this one was as beautiful and significant as they come. Sherri had created a keychain with charms attached, and each charm held special relevance. There was a guitar, a hippy peace sign, a charm with my birthstone, and a cross. The pendant on the chain was especially touching for me, as it closely resembled a necklace of my grandma's. Her necklace was very significant in my childhood, as she would let me wear it to make me feel so pretty and special. Now this amazing gift from Sherri brought together all the pieces to make a magnificent representation of the whole family knitted together. (She also gave one to my recently acquired siblings, Amanda and Jason... although Jason thought it was too girly and opted to create a tattoo that is manlier as a depiction, and my dad has it inked on his arm, too.) Oh, yeah and not to be left out... LeRoy was gifted a T-Shirt from Daytona. Which was more than meaningful to him!

This is actually the corner we sat in.

As dinner came to a close, LeRoy—who is a Marine's Marine and always so security conscious first and foremost, suggested we go somewhere quieter and talk. It had to be the hand of God working for him to make such a suggestion. So, we went back to the hotel that Jimmie and Sherri were staying at and we sat until after midnight just talking and crying and beginning to get to know each other. Once home, LeRoy and I talked late into the night. Mostly I talked and rambled on about how incredible the evening was and wondered what could possibly come next.

First Picture Together

Chapter Thirteen

We Are Family

Tuesday, March 15, 2011 at 5:00 AM
Subject: Thinking About You
To: Jessica
From: Jimmie

Good morning beautiful,

Just woke up thinking about you. You're my girl. Have a great day and find some time to take a nap!!!
Last night was amazing, you took my breath away. I am very excited and I know the future holds good things for me and you.

Have a great day today full of peace and smiles.

Love,
Jimmie

Tuesday, March 15, 2011 at 6:01 AM
Re: Thinking About You
To: Jimmie
From: Jessica

Good morning. We slept in. Just getting moving. Thank you for coming down here. The future looks to be pretty cool.

:-)

Tuesday, March 15, 2011 at 6:17 AM
Re: Thinking About You
To: Jessica
From: Jimmie

Jessica,

Cool, I'm glad you slept in…. I couldn't sleep so I've been up writing about you and my OUTSTANDING FAMILY! I'll be driving the next couple of days I'll talk with you when we stop and we stop a lot.

Here is the verse that was in my heart this morning, Ephesians 3:20 "Now unto him that is able to do exceeding abundantly above all that we ask or think, according to the power that work in us," We are right now experiencing/living what I'm calling "The Above Blessing" it's beyond my wildest dreams. I am a blessed man. Thank you for being you and making that happen for me.

Love you,
Jimmie

Tuesday, March 15, 2011 at 6:27 AM
Re: Thinking About You

To: Jimmie
From: Jessica

God is so amazing.

I'm so overwhelmed at the blessings He is giving. I'm excited for what comes next.

If you get a chance, poke around on my FB page. There are tons of pictures, some new, some old.

I've been poking around on yours for months
:-)

Tuesday, March 15, 2011 at 6:31 AM
Re: Thinking About You
　　　To: Jessica
From: Jimmie

Thanks sweetheart I will do some poking now....

Jimmie:

Sherri and I were so blessed and thrilled by our dinner the night before. We wanted to leave everything in Jessica and LeRoy's hands and let this all play out according to their timetable, we had every intention of heading home to Kansas City the next morning, but God had so much more in store for us. Before we hit the highway headed west in the White Pearl. Sherri insisted that we could not leave, saying. "It's just not right, we have to stay here and wait and see what happens next." She said, "This can't be all that there is, they have to know that this isn't, we met and now we're gone. We have to wait!"

Jessica:

Tuesday morning LeRoy suggested I invite them to lunch. That may seem benign and normal to most people, but LeRoy isn't most people and for him, it's not. We live far outside of Washington, D.C. so we have more green space than people. LeRoy as a particularly security minded introvert, wants in military terms a "defensible position." I knew again this whole lunch invitation idea must be from the Lord. Why else would my husband suggest this?

I messaged Jimmie and invited them to meet us for lunch at LeRoy's favorite after-work spot, Lord Hardwick's. We sat and talked again as if there was no time and not enough words in any language. As we were getting ready to leave, Jimmie mentioned that at some point they'd like to meet our boys. LeRoy said, "How about now? Why don't you follow Jessica home and meet them tonight." Again, I was shocked! Now at that time, my husband was working in Charlottesville, Virginia, we live in Maryland, nearly three hours away and he wasn't going to be there! So, my super-security-conscious marine husband says, "Yeah, it's okay! You can take strangers to our home and to meet our boys!"

On the way home to our house, we stopped by the church we were attending at the time so the first-time introductions could be made with the first two boys. Aaron was part of the youth group worship band rehearsal and was standing on the stage playing a guitar. As we walked in, Jimmie and Sherri wept at their first glimpse of my first-born. Jacob and Sherri become fast friends. My lovable little guy immediately fell into silliness and giggling. Sherri asked him, "What kind of gum do you like?" Jacob replied, "Hubba Bubba." Sherri laughed, "Me too," and pulled a pack from her purse. Their giggles quickly escalated into big belly laughs in the middle of the closing prayer echoing throughout the sanctuary. Troublemakers, both of them.

Aaron at church

Grammy and Jacob

Afterward, we went to our house where Matt and Seth are waiting. Just like their father, they were both somewhat stoic and hesitant. They were reserved as if to ask, *Why are you here? Are you for real? Don't you hurt my mom!* But it didn't take them long to jump all in, just like their younger brothers. It all became so natural, it was ridiculous. My sons have never called them Jimmie and Sherri, to them, they're Grammy and Pops. I still wasn't ready to let them leave after that night. We'd become family so I said, "You have to come back and sit at my table, 'cause that's what family does." Dinner for the following night was on.

Wednesday, March 16, 2011 at 9:22 AM
Subject: Menu
To: Jimmie
From: Jessica

Good morning. Thank you for that email this morning. You and Sherri both are going so far out of your way to make me welcome... my cup runneth over... :-)

So you can figure out what drinks you want to bring... :)
 Pan Fried Pork Chops with Apple Cranberry Chutney
Mixed greens salad with blue cheese, bacon and walnuts.

See you tonight. :)

Wednesday, March 16, 2011 at 9:42 AM
Re: Menu
To: Jessica
From: Jimmie

Shoot my cup has runneth over and now it's an ocean....

Menu is great... Looking forward to it.
Jimmie

Going Public

Social Media Post

Meet My Daughter Jessica
by Jimmie Bratcher on Wednesday, March 16, 2011 at 1:14pm

Dear Friends,

Sherri, Jason, Amanda and I would like for you, our friends, to share in our joy as we welcome into our family my daughter Jessica. There is a huge God story attached to this announcement that we will, in detail, reveal in the coming days.

No, I didn't have an affair. Jessica is from a relationship that I had before I met Sherri. The "details" will follow as soon as possible, all of us will be sharing something about our part in this remarkable event.

Please know I consider this to be one of the greatest experiences of my life. It is very deep, very spiritual, extremely personal and extremely wonderful. It has shown me much about myself, my family and God's great care and love for His children.

We welcome Jessica, her husband LeRoy and their sons Matt, Seth, Aaron & Jacob into our family.

We are extremely excited and honored to have them be part of us.

Peace & Blessings,

Jimmie, Sherri, Jason & Amanda

* * * * * * * * *

Wednesday, March 16, 2011 at 5:33 PM
Subject: A Little Something About Jessica
To: Jason, Amanda
From: Jimmie Bratcher

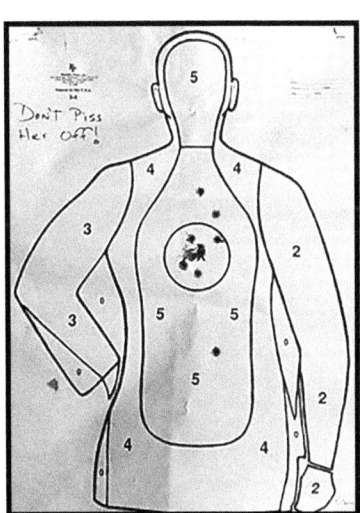

Here is a picture from the wall of LeRoy's garage that should give you a little insight about your sister!!!

Chapter Thirteen

The Great Ones

Thursday, March 17, 2011 at 8:14 AM
Subject: The Great Ones
To: Jason, Jessica Strong, Amanda Truxal, Sherri
From: Jimmie

To the Great Ones,
As a father I am maybe the proudest I have ever been of you all for a couple of reasons. First, because we are all together for the first time and I am so happy that Jessica is part of us. Second, because all of you have made it so easy for me to open up my heart to Jessica, that includes you too, Jessica. I am amazed at just how great you all are. You are the greatest people on the planet in my book and nothing will ever change that.

So, today I want you to do something for me, okay? I want you from this day forward to never doubt yourselves, never doubt your greatness. Never second guess that you are great and doing great things. Never doubt that you have all the abilities that you need to succeed. You are The Great Ones.

I love you,
Dad

Thursday, Mar 17, 2011 at 8:31 AM
Subject: For the Record
To: Jessica
From: Jimmie

Jessica,
Just for the record, this leaving you is a bunch of crap!!! Sherri said to tell you she loves you and misses you already.

From me, I can't imagine my life without you in it.

I love you, you're my girl,

Your Daddy!!!

Thursday, March 17, 2011 at 8:33 AM
Subject: Thanks Again
To: LeRoy
From: Jimmie

LeRoy,
Thanks again for allowing me into your life and home. Your family is great I like them all, you're a great father and a great husband. Thanks for letting me be part of your life.

Love,
Jimmie

Thursday, March 17, 2011 at 8:41 AM
Re: Thanks Again
To: Jimmie
From: LeRoy

Not a problem Jimmie. I enjoyed meeting you both and I'm glad you are so understanding of my feelings in all of this.

I look forward to seeing you again.
s/f
LeRoy

Thursday, March 17, 2011 at 9:04 AM
Subject Re: The Great Ones
To: Jimmie
From: Amanda

I want you to know as a father you are a GREAT ONE! and mom is a GREAT ONE... you have raised us to be loving, to roll with the punches to live life with our arms open wide saying... let's do this! To show love to those who wouldn't have experienced it before! For that I am SO very thankful! Love you guys SO much and I am so thankful you got to meet Jessica and that our lives are being completed!

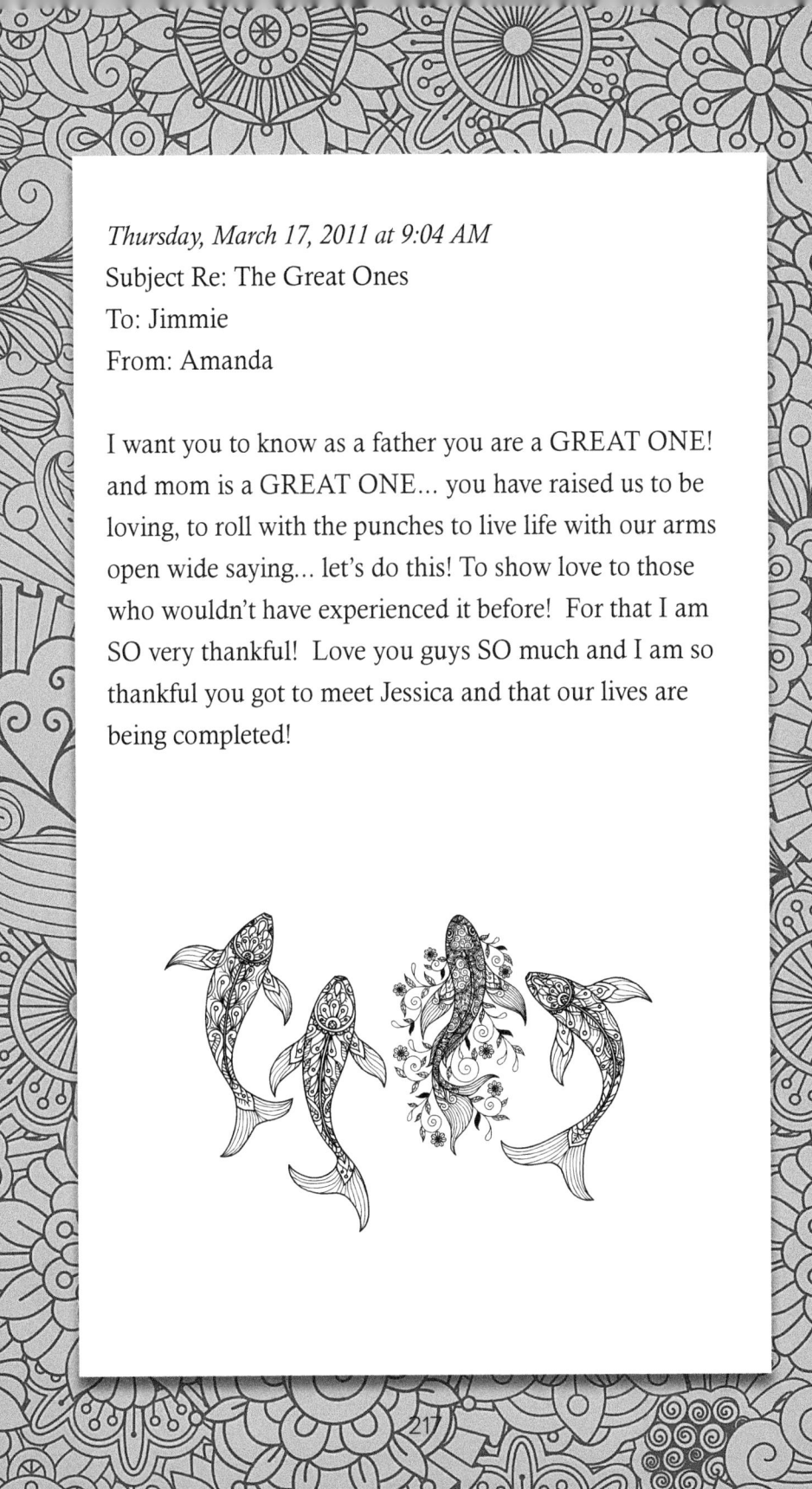

Thursday, March 17, 2011 at 10:02 AM
Re: For the Record
To: Jimmie
From: Jessica

Well, I feel the same way. I was completely pouting this morning and didn't get to work until an hour ago. I stayed home this morning to post something on Facebook, then decided to take Jacob to school instead of making him ride the bus.

I'm still pouting really. I don't want to be here. I'm sad you're going back. But I know we all have work to do.

Please drive safely and don't be too sad. We'll see each other again very soon. :)

Thursday, March 17, 2011 at 4:54pm
To: Jimmie
From: Jennifer (Jessica's Sister)

I'm so glad everything has worked out so well. I definitely cannot take credit for my part in all this. To God be all the glory!

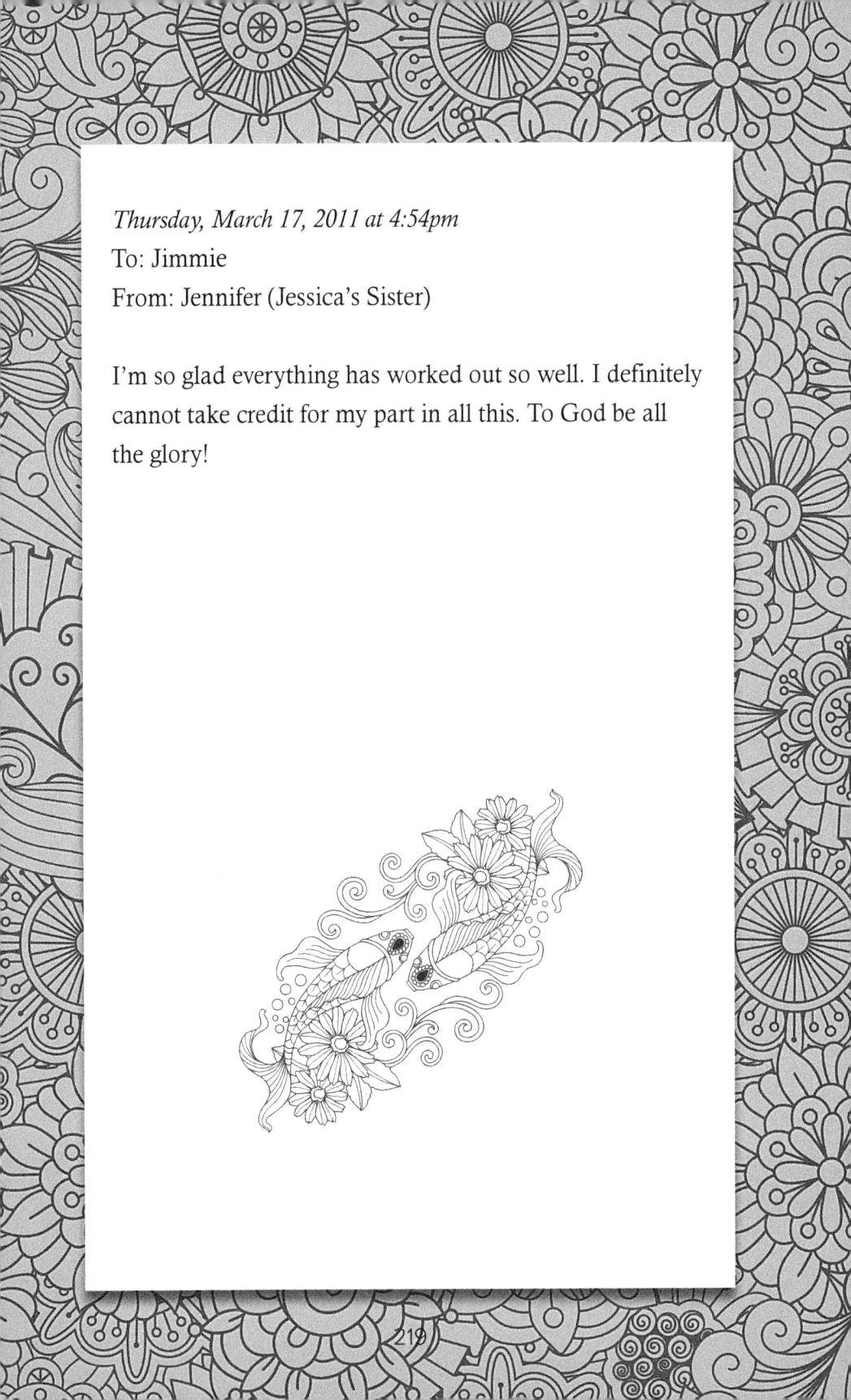

Thursday, March 17, 2011 at 10:38pm
To: Jimmie
From: Shelley (Jimmie's cousin)

Jimmie, I had a dream about 2 or 3 months ago, that you and Sherri had more grandchildren. I think I even shared that with Sherri. Wow, I wonder if God was trying to tell me something. Your story is beautiful. God is so good. Love you Cuz!

Friday, March 18, 2011
Subject: No Words
To: Jessica
From: Dad

Jessica,

I hope you have an absolutely wonderful day.

There are no words that I can find to describe the wonderful gift that you are to me.

I Love You,
Jimmie

Friday, March 18, 2011
Re: No Words
To: Jimmie
From: Jessica

Good morning. :)

I'm sitting in my office watching the sunrise bounce off the buildings. A guy who works for me came in to chat after being out all week for training. So, we chat a little about his projects and then he tells me about his sisters-in-law etc. As we start down the road talking about family, I tell him about my week, meeting you and Sherri and how wonderful everything has gone so far. He starts telling me his wife is adopted and is anxious to look for her birth mother. We talked about how important it is to have everything covered in prayer and to seek God's path before taking any steps on your own. Amazing... just inspiring...

I hope your drive is smooth and the traffic is light.
I've got a pretty full day ahead of me leading up to the dentist this afternoon. I probably won't be on here much, but I'll hop on as much as I can.

Love you... xoxo

Friday, March 18, 2011
To: Jessica
From: Jimmie
Re:re: No Words

Jessica,

You focus on work and stuff. I'll just be sitting in the White Pearl.

We just stopped at a Cracker Barrel for breakfast. Sherri has to have a morning salad?

The story is amazing and God is using you and I know that will only increase. Your advice to your co-worker is correct and very important.

In January we had a friend lose a daughter in a car wreck, it's very sad. She told us the story many years ago how at 17 she was raped and gave birth to a son who she put up for adoption. The day before her daughter's funeral a social worker contacted her and told her that her son who she had never before met was wanting to contact her. They met at just the right time. Just a God thing.
I am so changed by all of this. I am a different person than I was before 2/13. I am better than I was before.

Sherri and I talked last night late into the evening about the way we feel and about you. You're very special to me. I hope you never get tired of me telling you that.

Have a great day.
I Love You,
Jimmie

Friday, March 18, 2011
Re: No Words
To: Jimmie
From: Jessica

Hi. So work is hard to concentrate on when it's sunny at 70's. UGH...

It's going smoothly though; my worker bees are clickety clacking away on their projects and I'm waiting for them to bring them in for edits. Fortunately for them, I'm not motivated or I'd be pulling requirements for their next projects. I'll do that on Monday when it's only 50.

I ordered the charms for Jason and Amanda's key chains. I have a little reconfiguring to do when they get here so they're just right.

I got an email from Aunt Patsy with tons of pictures. Very cool! She's so sweet.

Morning Salad? That's a new one.... I'm easy... sausage, egg, cheese, multigrain toast... coffee, one truvia, half-n-half.

The number of people who are already asking about the story increases every day. I'm sure when we do put something more formal together it's going to be amazing. I can't wait to do that.

Hopefully your ride in the White Pearl is smooth and uneventful. I'm really looking forward to getting out of here today...

love you :)

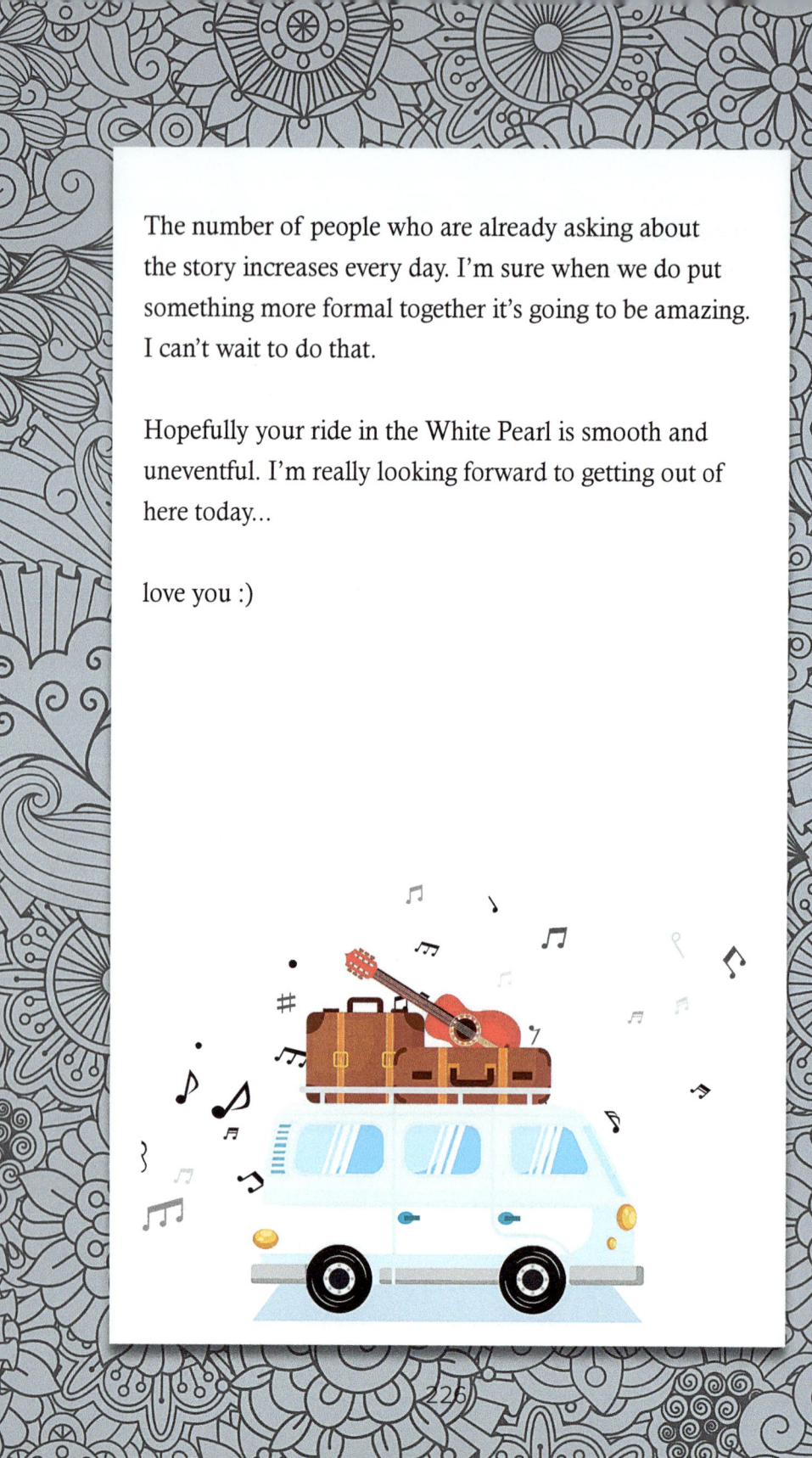

Social Media Blog Post
The Great Ones
by Jason Bratcher, March 21, 2011

For several days now, since the addition of a long unknown sister, this unit I call my family, the 3 of us have been getting emails just about every day from my dad simply titled, "The Great Ones." Each day he expresses just how blessed he is that we are in his life. They also encourage us to never quit and that no matter what circumstances may or may not come there is nothing that can hold us back. He tells us that we are to never doubt ourselves and to only believe and everything is at our fingertips. This has been such a good thing for me. I have always known that my dad has felt this way and he has never been shy about telling me or Amanda, it only serves to reason that with Jessica added into the mix he would do the same for her.

For much of my life I was raised under the belief that God was out to punish me for every sin that I committed or commit today or might commit in the future, and because God is not restrained by the bounds of time and space, that he already had been to my future and had already witnessed my past and watches my every current move and recorded every sin. If I was good enough and penitent enough then he might, through much fear and trembling, let me work out my salvation. This was called redemption and since I had accepted Jesus as my Savior I had bought my ticket to the fairground to at least be considered for the raffle, so I had a chance for this thing called grace, but I still had a lot of work to do if I was going to earn it, all the while hearing story after story of families that had been blessed because of the generations that had served God before them.

I have been witnessing a different type of salvation recently. You see a lot of people that read this will know the story that finds us here today. In the early 70s a guy and a girl met and fell in love and then came a little boy. The passionate hearts of these 2 corrupted by sin, drugs, alcohol, disease and religion manifested in great love and violent rages. They abused and beat each other and ended up driven apart by their urges and sin perverted hearts.

They, however, were brought back together in spite of themselves, by the belief of the young woman trying to change her perspective even though she was being told that her young lover was "not the saving type". Also pushing these 2 back together was the faith of the 2-year-old boy with his simple prayer of "I want my daddy back."

That fateful evening in December 1976 when God invaded their lives and changed EVERYTHING!
Now, I have always been told "be sure your sin will find you out", it will track you down and hunt you until you think you have finally out run it, then it will hit you when you least expect it and it will ruin everything good you might have in your life? I call B*!!S*#!

So, almost 40 years ago the boy I now call dad met a girl and as was the way of the 60/70s got wrapped up in the whole spirit of sex, drugs and rock-n-roll. From that short time in his life, I have been recently introduced to my older sister Jessica; she has taken her rightful place in our family in the last few weeks. Now at a glance, you would think the whole process of his sin finding him out was at work here. Not the way I see it. It seems that there is a little scripture that says "Believe in the Lord Jesus, and you will be saved--you and your household." What defines a household? Is it the people that live with you under your roof? I think it just might be more than that. You see on that night back in 1976 Jessica was not part of my unit that I knew as my family. However, when we finally learned of her and her family; husband LeRoy sons; Matt, Aaron; Seth and Jacob, one of the important details was that she was serving God not only her but her household as well.

You see, to me this did not look like the redemption that

You see, to me this did not look like the redemption that I grew up with, OH NO, to me this looks much more like the love of a lavish Father fulfilling His promise to a very honorable man and saving his WHOLE household.

Redemption is a complete work; the time lost, the hurt brought, the missed first steps through the birth of children. It's all redeemed, it's all restored. Does that sound like sinners in the hands of an angry God? I think not!

Time will tell just how deep this redemption and restoration has healed. I don't know the details yet, I haven't even yet heard my sister's voice or her laugh or seen the light in her eyes as she smiles. I don't know all the details of her life nor does she know the details of mine. I do know that because of a GREAT man, my life has been enhanced in ways I could have never imagined before. And because of his faith, this situation which we have all seen go really bad for other families, will not go that way for this family. My mom loves Jessica just as though she were here ALWAYS, it's so hard to explain but I feel the same, she was always here I just now see the tangible evidence of this.

I so look forward to meeting her soon. I am here today called A Great One because I was raised by The Great Ones. I am the result of a generational blessing. "We are the Kings and Queens of the Promise"!

Hope you all have a great Sunday.

Chapter Fourteen

Coming Home

On Memorial Day Weekend, 2011, we had our big Welcome Home Coming party for Jessica, LeRoy and the boys at our house. Sherri went all out...and I mean, *all out* with this party. She had the whole place decorated with balloons in the colors of all of their birthstones, quotes from the emails and texts that were exchanged in the reunion process were printed out and hung on the walls, and don't even get me started on the food! The whole clan was there to celebrate and extend the official welcome, even though everyone loved and considered them family immediately upon hearing the news a few months earlier. How many of you know that you don't have to actually meet family before you love them? In the words of my Aunt Fay, "Does she know we love her already?!"

The weekend was filled with so many moments of Mikaela, Zayne, & Jacob running around the yard, laughing and playing just like they'd known each other forever. At one point we were sitting on the deck and Jacob in his excitement to join us, ran right through the screen of the sliding glass door. He crash landed on the deck and we all busted out laughing at the site. I found my tools and rebuilt the screen door. Well wouldn't you know it, a few moments later here comes Zayne, crashing through the same screen. It was for sure a moment that only families get to experience. I think that may have been one of the moments that bound us together even tighter. Those moments, no matter how simple are to me, sacred.

May 29, 2011
Coming Home for the First Time

Jessica:

At some point in the party atmosphere of the weekend, Sherri suggested that Dad and I have some alone time together, so we escaped the hustle and bustle and got away for a ride in the White Pearl. Dad took me to our hometown where we both grew up in Liberty, Missouri. When we pulled up outside of where he grew up, I was in a bit of shock, I pointed to the house a half block away, (within sight), that I had lived in. In fact, two of the places that were home to me growing up were just a stone's throw from where he had lived. Except for the times I lived out of state, he and I were literally within blocks of one another, yet our paths never crossed except for the one time in the diner when I was thirteen. In meeting the extended family, I found out that my friend, Nikki, who I'd met in second grade and was good friends with during the time I lived in Liberty, was actually Dad's niece. (Remember, she was the friend that asked me what I'd do if I met my dad and I told her, "I'd punch him in the face!) I'd actually been to Nikki's home...Dad's sister Linda's home!

It was a small town, so our families were entwined. My uncles played baseball with Dad, and my mom's sister, Diane, went to high school with Dad's sister, Patsy. It seemed as though there were always connections there, even when we didn't know it, even when our lives never directly intersected.

This was also the weekend that we told our story publicly with my grandparents, Ralph and Charlotte, and sister Jennifer, LeRoy and the boys, Jason, Amanda and Aunt Patsy present. It was at The Rock of KC in Kansas City for the church's eighth anniversary celebration. They were doing a series titled "New Beginnings" and our story was a perfect fit.

Jimmie:

After Jessica and I were done telling our story, the whole family came up on the platform: Sherri, Amanda and her family, Jason, Jessica's grandparents and sister Jennifer, LeRoy and the boys. Grandma Charlotte just looked at us endearingly, busting at the seams over all that had happened and all God had done. And then something beyond words happened. I went to shake Grandpa Ralph's hand, and he put his hands on my shoulders and drew me near to him and said, "Jimmie, I'm proud of you. I haven't always been proud of you, but I'm proud of you for this." So, what do you do after something like that? You head to Arthur Bryant's for some barbeque!

Family together at The Rock of KC

Facebook Post
Welcome to the Family

By Jessica Strong on Friday, June 17, 2011 at 6:54 AM

(Written June 5th)
I'm sitting here in the quiet reeling from the incredible weekend with my new family. Welcomed by smiling faces and open arms. Hugs tight and long with so many joyful tears. Dad watching intently as I met Jason and Amanda for the first time, watching to see our reactions to each other.

Overwhelmingly, there is only peace and joy at this moment. And here is what I see... Dad and Mom (Jimmie and Sherri) are standing to the side, smiling faces; love filled hearts. My brother Jason is pensive, emotional and overwhelmed. My sister Amanda is quiet but loving completely. My brother-in-law Jonathan is quiet, tentative, but welcoming. Mikaela leaps; she is loving and intense. Zayne is quiet but watching me, quick to hug; equally quick to retreat.

Unseen at this moment are the heroes of this joyous occasion, I celebrate them. My mother and my grandparents, the Cottingham family. Throughout my years and my many trials, they were my cheerleaders, my support, and my safety net. Through the days when I was cute and bouncy; through the years when I was crazy, continuing through even now. As I chase the dreams of a professional, a mom, a Christian, they are there. They were always there when no one else was.

Through my sister attending a church where my father happened to play, through the support of all the Cottingham family and my mother's courage and sacrifice and prayer, I have this joyous opportunity to meet and know my father and siblings and be part of that wonderful family too. What happiness and blessings are pouring over my already full and blessed life!

Now, I'm getting back to my daily routine. In the past I would have called this my reality, but my reality has changed so drastically in recent months I'll call it routine. Now, I'm believing for a new reality; a reality that has fewer goodbyes and more daily routines that includes all that family, new and old.

I'm really missing my family now more than ever. I miss being in Liberty and the Kansas City area in a way I haven't missed it for a very long time. I have always had my mom, grandparents with one brother there. I have always been sad when I leave. This time it's harder when I didn't think that was possible. This time I have more to miss. Yet, while I left with a heavy heart, I am surrounded with great anticipation of the future.

Thanks to God are more than I could possibly express in words. The joy is endless and overwhelming. My heart is overflowing. To think the Creator of the heavens and earth could care about the details in the life of a sinner like me puts me on my knees in worship. It is He who has put the song in my heart, the skip in my step and the smile on my face. He knew my steps before I was created. And I am rejoicing because He does care about the details in this little girl's heart and the relationships in a family.

First Family Picture, left to right,
Amanda, Sherri, Jason, Jessica & Jimmie

PART THREE

Redemption:
The Rest of the Story

Chapter Fifteen

Miracles

Jimmie:

I've heard countless stories where families weren't reconciled because one spouse or the other said, "You're not bringing another child into this home. I will not share you with someone else." One of my close friends, a long-time pastor, and I were talking, as I told him the news of Jessica and her family, he asked this question. "How is Sherri?" He began to tell me a story very similar to ours, however, the husband was in fear that if he told his wife, she would divorce him. In no way would that be Sherri. She's been one of the biggest miracles on this journey. It was her great joy to welcome and knit Jessica and her family into ours and to have her in our home.

One day early in all of this, right after I had first emailed Jessica, Sherri and I were talking and she said to me, "You know, Jimmie, we have a great life. We have a great marriage and a great family. But, something's always been missing and this is it. Jessica, LeRoy and the boys are it.

Our daughter Amanda, without knowing what her mom said, echoed the exact same words:

Something's been missing, and this is it. Our son Jason had a different approach. He said, "You know I heard all those crazy stories about y'all before you came to Jesus, this doesn't surprise me! I'm surprised it didn't happen before now."

Jessica:

Sherri is every bit my mother as if she'd given birth to me herself. My husband calls her T-Mo—which is Technical Mom and he, too, calls Jimmie Dad. After LeRoy's mother passed away following her suffering from dementia, he began to call Sherri Mom. Nothing technical now, just Mom. God has knit us together as a family in a way that I didn't think was possible.

Jason and Amanda's love and graciousness are another miracle. Imagine being blindsided by a phone call from your dad dropping that kind of bomb! They were just as kind and welcoming as could be. We quickly became "real" siblings...by that, I mean posting pictures of me sleeping with my mouth open on Facebook like any younger brother should, having dart gun fights and teasing one another. It just doesn't get any more real than that.

We certainly can't leave LeRoy off the list of miracles. I've mentioned how out of his normal some of his actions were, and it's absolutely true. His response and support to me the whole way was, and is, all of God. Sherri and LeRoy stood in that restaurant parking lot, watching Dad and I hold one another and cry, and they surrounded us with more love than words can describe. I have no doubt that God used LeRoy to steadfastly walk me through the process of multiplying our family.

After we were united as a family, people would ask me, "Aren't you upset that he saw you when you were a 13-year-old and he knew you were his daughter, but didn't come back for you?" My indisputable answer is: No. I truly believe there were only two times when it would have ever worked for me, for us. Either when I was a very small girl, or when it actually happened. I certainly don't think that it would have been a good fit at all when I was thirteen. I believe I would have blown up the whole family at that time. I was such a train wreck as a teenager and young adult and I needed to work through so much in order to accept them in my life. I can look back and see where their faith and prayer for "Elaine's girl" covered me and protected me when I didn't have faith in my own life and didn't pray on my own. Like Dad and Mom said, *God knew the timing and when the right time came, it would all be okay.* In His time, it has been way more than okay.

Jimmie:

Sherri always says, "It's like God has woven us all together in a wonderful tapestry." That brings to mind the poem "Life is but a Weaving" also known as The Tapestry Poem written by Holocaust survivor Corrie ten Boom. God is the Master Weaver and He alone sees how all the threads of our lives come together to create a beautiful work of art. We tend to have only the view of the underside where it looks more like a mess of knots and strings than a magnificent picture. Yet, God sees it all from above, and at times, we get a glimpse of just how wonderfully He has taken each strand of our lives, the dark and light ones, the ones that are our favorites and the ones we don't like, and made something beautiful from them all.

Jessica:

Our first church service together was Easter Sunday, April 24, 2011, at my home church. In the morning when everyone else was still in bed, I came downstairs and was so excited, I felt like a five-year-old. Dad was up and I surprised him with a gift. It was a coffee mug with daddy names all over it and it was filled with my favorite candy bars—Zero candy bars. I had no way of knowing that it was his favorite candy bar, too! We were talking and I reached up and grabbed Dad by the face and said, "It's like you were always here." The thing that just wouldn't leave me was that it was like he was always a part of our lives. That's the best description of what it's like. All the void, all the pain, all the hurt, all the mistakes, all the wrong assumptions, God had the capacity to reach into our life and take those. Because we were willing to let Him take them.

Easter Service 2011 with Jessica's friend Jenn Legacy, LeRoy, Jessica & Jimmie

First Christmas: The KC Crew Invades DC

There was no way we were not celebrating Christmas 2011 together, and that was all there was to that. So we saved the money, bought the tickets and the entire KC Crew invaded Jessica's house. Even though they have a big house, there were still bodies everywhere.

Our first Christmas together!

As the festivities began it only took a moment to know that these folks are crazy! You know it's a DNA thing! Christmas Eve was homemade pizza. Meaning everyone had their own individual pizza that me and LeRoy cooked on the grill. When the dust settled, we'd grilled something like sixteen of those bad boys. We laughed, we told endless stories, the grandkids were all over the place, and it was fantastic. "Time for church." Jessica said. So Matt and Aaron decided that sombreros would be the appropriate attire! When we arrived at church Matt locked arms with Grammy and escorted her into the church. It is a fabulous memory.

Redeeming The Past:

Jimmie:

Have you ever read Matthew Chapter One in the Bible? The genealogy of Jesus. If you've tried I bet you're like me and gazed at the page in a blank stare thinking, who are these people and why are they important to me? Well, they may not seem important to us, however, they are very important to The Father. These passages speak to us about how He tracks our heritage with great detail and love; with every one of us being sacred to Him.

God's power is limitless. Yet, many times we simply limit the power of God in our lives. It is at times beyond our intellect and only with our hearts that we can understand it. That is what happened to me on this Easter Sunday morning.

You see, I assumed that I qualified for God's blessings in my life starting on December 19, 1976, the day I believed in Jesus, and then forward. Where I limited His power was I had not fully understood that He is not bound by time. He created time for us but it is never a limitation for Him. I had limited Him until He reached into my past, to a time when I didn't know or regard Him at all, and started doing what He does, redeeming things! As Jessica walked away that Easter morning my heart opened to His voice as I heard these words: *"Jimmie I've been faithful to your seed, even when you were not."* Suddenly, I understood that when He promised to be faithful to my children, it included the wonderful young woman that had just given me this very special gift. He reached back into my life and was as He is, faithful. He calls it "redeeming the time".

When Jessica said, "Daddy, it's just like you were always here," she described exactly how it was and is to this day. Through His power He redeemed all of that time that we lost, and filled our hearts as if we hadn't ever missed a day together. It is one of the wildest things I have ever experienced. At times I am in awe and wonder just how He could bless my family so much.

As a father, I can't tell you how grateful I am that I have the experience of a God who loves me and isn't afraid of my mistakes.

Redeeming The Present: Two Out of Three Ain't Bad!

Jimmie:

When all this started to unfold I asked The Lord, "What do I do?" His answer, *"Love her."* When those words entered my heart I knew exactly what to do. You see, love isn't about what we receive, it is about what we give. I knew how to love Sherri, Jason, Amanda, and my grandkids, and now my heart was ready to do the same with Jessica, LeRoy and the boys.

One of the first things that Sherri said to Jessica and LeRoy the evening that we met was, "We don't want anything from you, we are just grateful that you would allow us into your lives." I say it like this. Love is not demanding, love is giving. Love is an action that if true, never demands a response. It does have to begin somewhere and I say, "Let it start with me."

Do Something

When it's your family that's been hurt and offended, when it's you that's been abandoned, rejected, or needing forgiveness, how will you act? What will you do? When everything's right for you to apply the truth in love towards those who hurt you or those who need to be forgiven, what will you do?

We know in talking to so many families that fear, and selfishness are the things that keep us separate. So, we ask you to *do something*. Stop living in the hurt of the past. You can allow God to redeem the time and to create an opportunity to heal your relationships. You can embrace faith instead of fear. Have enough confidence in the power of love to begin to make a different experience. You can believe that things can be different, because all things are possible.

Jessica:

We all live with assumptions...most of them are bad. I lived for years with a bad assumption that I was unloved, unwanted, abandoned and neglected. And out of fear for something different, that I wasn't enough, I wasn't good enough, I allowed that to stay there. But the reality is, our God is bigger than that. He cared enough about you to number the hairs on your head. He knows everything about you. He created everything about you. So, stop living in those bad assumptions with those fears and allowing those fears to paralyze you. Those fears keep you stationary and keep you from becoming who He designed you to be. You have to take a step in faith to not be afraid, to allow God to wipe those away. To recognize that I am loved. I'm not neglected, I'm not abandoned. I'm exactly who He wants me to be and exactly who He designed me to be, right here, right now, today, in this moment. Stop living in fear and allow God to start that process of forgiveness.

Then, regardless of the outcome, forgive yourself. Ah, this may be the hardest one, I know it was for me. "How could I have done this to my own child?" Honestly I still shake my head in amazement that I did this terrible thing to one of my children. Jessica taught me this on the first day we met and I asked her to forgive me, she said. "We can't change the past, so we're cool." She forgave me, now I had to forgive myself. I have to admit it took me awhile. God had forgiven me, my family forgave me, and Jessica forgave me. It was now time for me to forgive myself. To let go of the past and the past regret, and live in the present and from there build our family's future.

I know that this isn't easy. However, we wrote this book, sharing with you our family's most precious moments in the hope of helping you find the faith that you need to face your fears and face each other and love one another.

Peace to you,
from our family!